ELEVEN MONTHS TO
FREEDOM

A German POW's Unlikely Escape from Siberia in 1915

Dwight R. Messimer

Naval Institute Press
Annapolis, Maryland

This book has been brought to publication with
the generous assistance of Marguerite and Gerry Lenfest.

Naval Institute Press
291 Wood Road
Annapolis, MD 21402

Library of Congress Cataloging-in-Publication Data
Names: Messimer, Dwight R., date author.
Title: Eleven months to freedom : a German POW's unlikely escape from Sibe-
    ria in 1915 / Dwight R. Messimer.
Description: Annapolis, Maryland : Naval Institute Press, [2016] | Includes
    bibliographical references and index.
Identifiers: LCCN 2016015616 (print) | LCCN 2016015916 (ebook) | ISBN
    9781682470657 (hardcover : alk. paper) | ISBN 9781682470664 (ePub) |
    ISBN 9781682470664 (ePDF) | ISBN 9781682470664 (mobi)
Subjects: LCSH: Killinger, Erich, 1893–1977. | Prisoners of war—Germany—
    Biography. | Prisoners of war—Russia—Biography. | Germany. Krieg-
    smarine—Officers—Biography. | World War, 1914–1918—Prisoners and
    prisons, Russian. | Escapes—History—20th century. | Germany. Luft-
    waffe—Officers—Biography. | Military interrogation—Germany—Ober-
    ursel. | World War, 1939–1945—Prisoners and prisons, German. | Voyages
    around the world.
Classification: LCC D627.R8 M38 2016 (print) | LCC D627.R8 (ebook) | DDC
    940.4/7247092 [B] —dc23
LC record available at https://lccn.loc.gov/2016015616

All photos are from the author's collection.
Maps 1 through 5 created by Christopher Robinson.

24 23 22 21 20 19 18 17 16   9 8 7 6 5 4 3 2 1
First printing

To John Schuster,
a great story teller and a terrific host

Contents

Maps

Comparative Ranks in the U.S. Navy
and the Imperial German Navy in World War I

U.S. NAVY	IMPERIAL GERMAN NAVY
Admiral	Admiral
Vice Admiral	Vizeadmiral
Rear Admiral	Kontreadmiral
Captain	Kapitän zur See
Commander	Fregattenkapitän
Lieutenant Commander	Korvettenkapitän
Lieutenant	Kapitänleutnant
Lieutenant (Junior Grade)	Oberleutnant zur See
Ensign	Leutnant zur See
Midshipman	Fähnrich zur See

Source: From "Table of Comparative Ranks in Different Navies," Department of Modern Languages, U.S. Naval Academy, *Spanish Nautical Phrase Book and Reader* (Annapolis: U.S. Naval Institute, 1914).

ERICH KILLINGER

The airplane was canted sharply to the right, its wingtip in the water, the right float slowly sinking. The weather was cold and clear, the water temperature near freezing. Two German naval aviators, soaked to the skin, sat precariously atop the undamaged left pontoon, shivering. Land was less than a mile away, but there was no hope for rescue from that direction—at least not the sort of rescue they wanted.

Too cold to talk, they stared out at the empty Baltic hoping a ship would materialize. None came. Fähnrich zur See Erich Killinger, who had celebrated his twenty-second birthday just three weeks earlier, could not know that he was about to embark on a very long journey that would take him halfway around the world before he returned to Germany.[1]

Erich Walter Emil Killinger was born on 21 March 1893 in Schönau, near Wiesental, about thirty miles southwest of Heidelberg in the Grand Duchy of Baden. His father, Emil Killinger, was a member of the privy council appointed to advise Grand Duke Friedrich I of Baden (1856–1907) and his successor, Friedrich II (1907–18). His mother, the former Elisabeth Helfrich, was a typical upper-class German housewife and mother who doted on her son. Shortly after Erich was born his family moved to Heidelberg.[2]

Killinger was born at a time when German nationalism was at its height and Germany, under Kaiser Wilhelm II, was developing an aggressive foreign policy. Four years after Killinger's birth, the Kaiser appointed Kontreadmiral Alfred Peter von Tirpitz secretary of state for the navy (Staatssekretär des Reichsmarineamt), an appointment that launched a massive expansion of the Imperial German Navy. Killinger thus grew up in a society in which military service was expected of all healthy males and the Imperial Navy carried the banner for Germany's foreign policy.

Emil Killinger's position as a trusted adviser to the Grand Duke put the Killingers among the social upper crust—not aristocrats, but the upper gentry—and Erich enjoyed the advantages of growing up in a fairly well-to-do, socially well-placed family. His upbringing underscored the importance of maintaining high principles and character, and produced a slightly superior attitude that became more pronounced after he was commissioned an officer in the German navy.

Erich scrupulously showed fellow members of the German officer class the respect and deference due to each man's rank, but his sense of class superiority became apparent when he interacted with people outside his class. His openly displayed sense of superiority caused many people to view him as a cold fish, which he was not, although he tended to view things as either black or white. He was exceptionally intelligent, had a strong sense of duty and honor, and held a firm belief in an orderly society that was commanded from the top. He was, in short, a royalist.

Killinger's sense of entitlement also showed in his attitude that regulations, rules, and orders could be bent or ignored to suit himself. He had almost no sense of humor, and though he was certainly not a loner, he did not make close friends easily.

At eighteen, Erich was six feet, three inches tall with blond hair and blue eyes. He was an avid hiker, which prepared him well for what lay ahead in 1915 and 1916. He was also reasonably attractive, well groomed, and thoroughly trained in social graces. These qualities, combined with a natural ability to make small talk, allowed him to easily mingle with mixed company, especially company that included young women, and he played the role of a bon vivant whenever the opportunity presented itself. He was intelligent, an excellent student, and had a talent for learning languages. By the time he had completed his public education in 1910 and passed his university qualification exam (*Abitur*) he was fluent in English and French.

Erich studied law and economics at Kings College in London, the University of Heidelberg, and at universities in Hamburg and Berlin. But a career in law or economics was not what he had in mind, and he spent little time at each university. On 1 April 1913 he gave up his university studies altogether and entered the Imperial Navy's officers' school at Mürwik in Flensburg. He was a member of Crew IV/13, one of 293 cadets organized in 4 sections. Each section was assigned to one of the five *Victoria Louise*–class cruisers that entered service in 1898 and 1899: SMS *Victoria Louise*,

SMS *Herta*, SMS *Freya*, SMS *Hansa,* and SMS *Vineta*. Killinger's section was assigned to the *Vineta* under Kapitän zur See Wilhelm Adelung.[3]

The Imperial Navy offered glamour and glory at sea, but the German army, known as the *Herr,* was the nation's real muscle, and every German armed forces recruit, regardless of which service branch he entered or what he intended to be—officer or enlisted man—went through infantry training before he did anything else. From 1 April until 15 May 1913 Killinger and his fellow sea cadets were trained as infantrymen with heavy doses of close-order drill, rifle practice, and guard duty. Basic infantry training was followed by ten and a half months of practical seamanship training on board the *Vineta*. The *Vineta* returned to Mürwik in late March 1914, and on 1 April Killinger started his classroom work. On 3 April, along with his classmates, he was promoted to Fähnrich zur See.

Under normal circumstances the classroom work would have lasted twelve months and ended on 31 March 1915, at which time the midshipmen would have been assigned to High Seas Fleet units for several months before being promoted to Leutnant zur See, a rank equivalent to ensign in the U.S. Navy. But on 28 June 1914, in Sarajevo, Bosnia, Gavrilo Princip murdered Archduke Franz Ferdinand of Austria and the Archduke's wife, Sophie, Duchess of Hohenberg, and everything changed.

On 15 July, during the "tension period" (*Periode der Spannungen*) that preceded the declaration of war, the school commandant closed the school and sent the midshipmen home for a thirty-day leave before being assigned to the High Seas Fleet. Before releasing them, he gave the cadets strict orders to remain in Germany. He was particularly adamant that they were not to go into Austria.

Killinger disregarded the orders, convinced that the commandant would not find out, and along with his civilian friend Walter Bartolome went directly to Austria for a hiking holiday in the Tyrol Mountains. His family knew where he was, he reasoned, so there was nothing to worry about. That willful disobedience was an early indication that he was a risk taker whose judgment was not always sound.

On 28 July, while he and Walter were tramping through the Alps singing *Oh du schöner Westerwald* and quaffing beer in the *Gasthaus,* Austria-Hungary declared war on Serbia; Russia started mobilizing the next day. The two men were still happily oblivious when Germany declared war on Russia four days later on 1 August. On that day a telegram from the school arrived at the Killinger home in Heidelberg ordering Erich to return to the school immediately. His mother dutifully sent a telegram to the Austrian telegraph office near where Killinger and his friend were hiking, informing him that the school wanted him to come back immediately. She said nothing about a war starting. The following day, 2 August, an Austrian telegram deliveryman trudged four hours up the mountain to the inn where Killinger and Bartolome were registered, only to find that the two young men were out hiking. The telegraph official sighed, pocketed the telegram, and trudged back down the mountain.

When the two hikers strolled into the inn the next afternoon, 3 August, the innkeeper told Killinger that a telegram was waiting for him at the telegraph office. That could not be good news. Still unaware that Germany was at war, Killinger immediately assumed that the school commandant had found out about his deliberate disobedience and that his embryonic naval career was rapidly sinking. He hurried upstairs to his room, jammed his clothes into his rucksack, and started down the mountain in the dark. He made the usual four-hour hike in three hours, fretting all the way that the telegraph office would be closed when he got there.

The telegraph office was not only open when he arrived, it was jammed with Austrian reservists picking up their mobilization orders. Now alarmed beyond measure, Killinger grabbed the envelope from the agent's hand, ripped it open, and read the bland message from his mother: "Due to the school starting earlier, you are to return immediately." Despite the absence of urgency in his mother's message, the activity around him made it clear that a state of urgency did exist. It was now after 8 p.m. on 3 August, and he finally knew that Austria was at war. He was still unaware of Germany's declaration of war on Russia, but he knew that if Germany was not at war, it soon would be. And instead of being at his post in Flensburg he was in Austria, where his commandant had specifically forbidden him to go. His feeling of impending doom was palpable.

He rushed out of the telegraph office and ran across the street to the train station, hoping to catch a late train to Heidelberg, but the next train was not scheduled to depart until 5:30 a.m. on 4 August, to arrive in Heidelberg that same evening. If the train was on time, he could make the night connection to Flensburg and arrive there on the morning of 5 August.

But his problems were just starting. The Austrian rail system was overwhelmed with demands for extra trains. The stationmaster announced that extra trains had been added, but they were packed beyond capacity and experiencing unexpected delays. Killinger was already late, and the news fed his growing fear that he would be even more overdue when he finally arrived in Flensburg.

At midmorning on 4 August he managed to board a train to Hamburg, only to learn upon arriving that there would not be a train to Flensburg for several hours. It was now the evening of 4 August, and a morning arrival in Flensburg on 5 August was a pipe dream. He tried unsuccessfully to hire a car and driver to take him to Flensburg that night, but he was stuck. All he could do was wait, sweating bullets as time crept by. Had he known then that Great Britain had already declared war on Germany, he might have considered throwing himself under a train.

He was an emotional wreck when he finally arrived in Flensburg the following afternoon and reported to the commandant's office. To his utter surprise and enormous relief, no one asked why he was late or where he had been between 1 and 5 August. The duty clerk checked off his name, told him to find a berth in the barracks, and handed him a dining hall pass. If there is a single outstanding feature of Killinger's wartime service, it is his sheer good luck; at crucial moments his salvation was a matter of pure serendipity.

The declaration of war that caused the immediate mobilization of the German armed forces had created a chaos in which one midshipman more or less made absolutely no difference. Having dodged that bullet, his despair turned into buoyant optimism, and Killinger fully expected an immediate assignment to a modern cruiser. But glory at sea is generally reserved for the truly deserving. Since he was not yet considered deserving, he joined the ranks of those who served by swabbing decks, polishing brass, and marching to and from other time-occupying assignments while waiting.

On the fourth day after his return the school commandant called a general muster and handed out assignments. Each midshipman received a card about the size of a standard playing card on which was stamped his next duty station. Most of the young men were sent to the school cruisers for deployment as part of the Baltic Coastal Defense Division under Kontreadmiral Gisbert Jasper. A few, including Killinger's classmate Günther Schwarz, went to Johannisthal near Berlin for training as aerial observers in the navy's aviation section, and others were sent to the High Seas Fleet.[4]

Killinger eagerly turned over his card, expecting to see a cruiser's name. A name *was* stamped on the card, but it was not a cruiser. In fact, it was not even a ship. It was Wilhelmshaven. He looked at the puzzled young men around him who had received similar assignments. "What does Wilhelmshaven mean?" they were asking themselves and each other. Though they had their assignments, the waiting was not quite over. There was still the matter of finding a train to take them to the naval base, and the priority assigned to a bunch of midshipmen was somewhere between very low and nonexistent.

When the train pulled into Wilhelmshaven's main station, the midshipmen found the platforms crowded with recruits and reservists, all headed toward the station's exits. The midshipmen climbed down from the train and joined the throng as it flowed through the wide double doors onto the street outside, where they were formed into groups to be marched into the naval base.

Killinger and his classmates quickly learned that even among raw recruits midshipmen drew little water. That reality was underscored when he and the other midshipmen were assigned to their temporary quarters in a riding hall. The single enormous, open bay was filled with bunks stacked three high and equipped with straw-filled mattresses. The midshipmen spent several miserable days in the hall spreading rumors, playing cards, and griping about their situation while waiting for something to happen. Killinger later said that it "seemed they had forgotten the poor midshipmen."

Several days later he and two other midshipmen received written orders to report to the first officer on SMS *Berlin*, a light cruiser that was undergoing conversion. The officer who handed them the orders did not know exactly where the cruiser was berthed and told the three midshipmen to ask around. Encouraged to know that his assigned ship was a light cruiser, Killinger set out with his mates to find her. After nearly three hours, they did. The *Berlin*'s decks were swarming with workers and enveloped in hoses and lines, and equipment was stacked everywhere.

His disappointment was staggering. Instead of the modern light cruiser he was expecting, the *Berlin* was "an old crate that would require weeks before she was ready for sea." She was a *Bremen*-class light cruiser that had been commissioned in 1905, but her design was already outdated, and she was useful only for coastal patrol and picket boat duty. The *Berlin* was assigned to the Third Harbor Flotilla, which comprised three obsolescent light cruisers, four gunboats, seven torpedo boats, and two auxiliary minesweeping divisions. The unit operated out of Wilhelmshaven to patrol the waters off the mouths of the Jade and the Weser, an assignment that rarely took the ships out of sight of land.

Like many young German men who were called up or volunteered for the armed services in August 1914, Killinger was eager to go. But his assignment to coastal patrol and picket duty was an enormous disappointment. He wanted to see action before the war was over, and as most twenty-one-year-old German males in 1914 did, he expected the war to end quickly.

When Britain declared war on Germany on 4 August, Germany had been unified for just forty-three years, less than an average lifetime. During the seven years from 1864 to 1871, Prussia fought three short wars, starting with a ten-month campaign against Denmark that brought Schleswig-Holstein under Prussian control. Austria was next in July 1866 in what became known as the Seven Weeks' War, which added twenty-two German states to the union. The third and most dramatic war was fought against France from 19 July 1870 to 10 May 1871 and ended with Germany acquiring major parts of Alsace and Lorraine and raising the now-unified Germany to the status of the most powerful industrial state in Europe. In all three wars, Prussian weapons, training, and discipline overwhelmed the opponents. It is no wonder that the Germans expected this new war to be over by Christmas 1914.

Immediately after he reported to the *Berlin*'s first officer and was detailed along with the other midshipmen to chip paint and pick rust, Killinger started looking for a way to get off the ship. He was still there on 30 August when the old cruiser went to sea to take up her picket station off the outer Jade. Throughout his time on board the *Berlin*, Killinger persisted in asking for an assignment that he thought would offer a better chance of seeing combat. He had several choices, the least exciting to him being naval aviation.

The German army had a respectable air force in August 1914, but the German navy's air arm was only slightly beyond the experimental stage. The Imperial Navy had only ten heavier-than-air (HTA) aircraft in its entire inventory, each of a different design and none suited for combat in any capacity. The navy had been constructing airfields for HTA aircraft since 1913, and several fields were ready to receive them, but few aircraft of any kind were available until many months after the war started. Nevertheless, Killinger requested assignment to naval aviation. The naval air arm was starting to expand, and it at least offered a chance to fly over the enemy, both ashore and at sea.

The Imperial Navy's leadership intended to build an air arm capable of overwater and overland reconnaissance and battlefield area observation, and recognized the need for air superiority and airfield defense fighters. But they faced two problems: lack of money and the German aviation industry's preference for army contracts over navy contracts. The German industry's reluctance to provide naval aircraft designs was at least in part due to the fact that they were more difficult to build and more expensive than land-based army airplanes.

At the outbreak of the war, the Imperial Navy was favoring lighter-than-air (LTA) aircraft called "airships" rather than airplanes for its air arm, but there were plans for using HTA aircraft in both observation and attack roles. As it worked out, German naval aviators, including Killinger, saw plenty of action during the war in both types of aircraft.[5]

By the time he submitted his request Killinger had discovered that a midshipman was at the bottom of the list for any assignment except the one he now held, but the old saying that the squeaky wheel gets the grease is true, and in September the navy sent him to the naval aerial observers' school at Johannisthal in Berlin to be trained as an aerial observer.

ERICH GOES TO WAR

8 September 1914–5 April 1915

The airfield at Johannisthal, outside Berlin, was the home of German military aviation from 1908 to the end of World War I. Several aero engine, aero design, and aircraft manufacturing companies were located there, including the Wright Flying Machine Company, which became Luftfahrt Flugzeug Gesellschaft (LFG); Zeppelin; AGO Flugzeugwerke; Albatros-Flugzeugwerke; Rumpler; and Luftverkehrs GmbH, a builder of dirigibles and airplanes. In 1909 the German army authorized the sale of the Johannisthal flying field to Arthur Müller's Johannisthal Flugplatz Gesellschaft and paid Müller twenty thousand marks annually for unlimited use of the field and facilities. Because the companies located at the airfield all had government contracts, they provided factory aircraft for training army and navy pilots and observers. The service for which the pilot or observer trainee would be flying wrote the training syllabus.[1]

Each observer was paired with an experienced naval aviator with whom he would remain when both were assigned to an active squadron. Killinger was fortunate to be paired with Oberleutnant zur See Karl von Gorrissen from Baden, who had been in the navy since 3 April 1907 and qualified as a pilot on 9 April 1912. His German pilot's license number 178 established him as an aviation pioneer, and he had been awarded the Prussian Order of the Crown, Fourth Class, for his flying skill before the war. He was five years older than Killinger, and his father, like Killinger's father, held a responsible government position.[2]

Von Gorrissen and Killinger trained in the Rumpler 4B-11, an unarmed reconnaissance airplane equipped with a six-cylinder inline, water-cooled Benz 100-horsepower engine. In 1914 the navy bought eight improved 4B-12s that were equipped with floats and were powered by a 150-horsepower Benz engine that could lift a 705-pound payload. The navy assigned numbers 49–51 and 86–90 to the new airplanes. After the war started, the navy added bomb racks that would hold a 100-pound bomb load. At that time the bomb load choice was limited to a single 100-pound bomb or ten 10-pound bombs. Although it was already obsolescent, the Rumpler 4B was rugged and reliable, and the lack of defensive armament was not a drawback because at the time there was no fighter opposition in the operations area to which they were going—the Baltic.[3]

When Killinger arrived at Johannisthal on Tuesday, 8 September 1914, he was already earmarked for assignment to the Baltic naval force under Grossadmiral Heinrich Prince of Prussia, younger brother of Kaiser Wilhelm II. The Baltic was a secondary theater of operations that did not involve heroic fleet actions, being more directed at laying mine-fields, minesweeping, shore bombardments, and "demonstrations" at the entrance to the Gulf of Finland. The ships assigned to the Baltic force were second-class units, obsolete, or at least obsolescent, and manned almost entirely by reservists.[4]

German naval aviation likewise had little military value in August and September 1914, because the flyers had little flight experience and no war training. On 19 August there were no serviceable aircraft at the navy's Holtenau and Warnemünde air stations, and only one at Putzig; in fact, there were only twenty airplanes in the entire Baltic area, nearly all of them unready for service.[5]

On 2 October Killinger and von Gorrissen left Johannisthal for the naval air station at Putzig, the headquarters for the newly created German naval air arm. Built in 1913, Putzig was on the west side of the entrance to Danzig Bay, twenty-eight statute miles north of the city of Danzig. Ober-leutnant zur See Clifford von Tempsky, who had been a pilot since November 1913, had been in command of Putzig since 2 August. Killinger found a classmate there, Günther Schwarz, whose pilot was an enlisted man, Oberbootsmannsmaat (Petty Officer 2nd Class) Rolf Bachmann; both had arrived at Putzig in September.

Putzig was equipped with the upgraded Rumpler 4B-12s, and von Gorrissen and Killinger were assigned to number 51, one of the original eight planes purchased. The trainees flew training missions over the Gulf

Map 1 Overview of the East Prussia theater, August 1914–April 1915

Based on Rudolph Firle, *Der Krieg in der Ostsee*, vol. 1 (Berlin: Verlag E. S. Mittler & Sohn, 1921), Karte 1.

of Danzig and the central Baltic, and were sometimes sent on real missions to look for submarines and minefields. During their time at Putzig, the ground war in East Prussia was going well for the Germans.

Sixteen days after Germany declared war on Russia on 1 August, General Paul von Rennenkampf's First Army invaded East Prussia. Initially the Russian offensive went well, forcing the Germans back toward Königsberg. General Alexander Samsonov's Second Army invaded from the south, hoping to trap the German Eighth Army under Generaloberst Paul von Hindenburg between the two Russian armies. Instead, the Eighth Army turned west and attacked the Russian Second Army at Tannenberg on 26 August, even though the Russian force had a numerical superiority of about two to one. The battle lasted until 30 August and ended in the almost complete destruction of the Russian Second Army, which suffered as many as 3,000 killed and 92,000 taken prisoner.[6]

Although von Hindenburg's force had been unable to push the Russians out of Germany, the victory had bolstered German morale and demoralized the Russians. Following the Battle of Tannenberg, Rennenkampf's First Army suffered a crushing defeat at the First Battle of the

Masurian Lakes, fought from 9 to 14 September. Rennenkamp's force was virtually destroyed, suffering approximately 50,000 casualties and as many as 10,000 taken prisoner. The victory drove the Russians back all along the front, and ultimately back into Russia.

When Killinger and von Gorrissen arrived at Putzig, the First Battle of the Masurian Lakes was still being fought and the Russians were retreating all along the front. On 12 September the German Admiralty Staff sent a telegram to Grossadmiral Prince Heinrich, himself a pioneer pilot, directing him to support the army in disrupting the Russian retreat by destroying the pontoon bridges across the Memel River between Memel and Tilsit.[7]

The problem with the order was that the Baltic fleet had no ships capable of navigating the Memel River beyond Memel. The only possible solution was to use Rumpler 4Bs from the naval air station at Putzig to bomb the bridges. The Rumpler 4Bs had the necessary range to reach the pontoon bridges and return to Putzig, but their ability to destroy the bridges was questionable. It was a moot issue anyway, because all the airplanes at Putzig were currently out of service. As things worked out, it did not matter because German cavalry entered Tilsit on 13 September and reported that there were no enemy forces present between Tilsit and Memel.

While the land war was going in Germany's favor, the sea war in the Baltic did not seem to be going anywhere. Both the Germans and the Russians believed that their forces were inferior to their enemy's, and both were in some areas correct. Because the German Admiralty viewed naval operations in the Baltic as a sideshow, they sent second-rate ships there. But the ships were adequate for the task of sealing up the Russian fleet in the Gulf of Finland and keeping the Baltic open for trade with the Nordic states.[8]

The Russians, for their part, were still smarting from their defeat in the Russo-Japanese War and were happy to remain bottled up in the Gulf of Finland. Russia's Baltic Fleet was focused on commanding the Gulf of Finland and the Bay of Riga with the purpose of defending St. Petersburg, nothing more. The tsar made that clear when he told his Baltic Fleet commander, Admiral Nikolai Ottovich von Essen, "We do not want a second Tsushima."[9]

The strategies the Germans and Russians adopted in the Baltic did not make for the sort of action-packed theater of operations that Killinger had in mind when he got himself transferred to the naval air arm. But there were occasional surprises and flaps that gave him reason to hope that things would start to heat up.

The first cause for hope was the assignment of Kontreadmiral Ehler Behring to the newly created post of chief of special operations. The forty-nine-year-old Behring was said to be a man of great daring, seamanship, and military experience. Grossadmiral Prince Heinrich had created the post for Behring "in order to have an officer who was free of bureaucratic red tape associated with administration and logistics, and thus free to devote his energies to fighting the enemy." Kontreadmiral Behring's other title was "detached admiral," meaning that he had no assigned command of his own and had to draw on the other divisions for ships and manpower to accomplish his missions.[10] Kontreadmiral Behring conducted several operations intended to draw the Russians out of the Gulf of Finland, and these small skirmishes resulted in losses to both sides, but it was not until September and October that events opened the door for Killinger to become involved.

During the night of 1–2 September 1914 the light cruiser SMS *Augsburg* and the torpedo boat SMS *V25* encountered two Russian cruisers and three large destroyers northeast of Gotland Island, well outside the Gulf of Finland. Though outgunned and outclassed by the five Russian warships, the *Augsburg* called for help and prepared to do battle. But to the Germans' surprise, and probably relief, the Russians turned tail and sped off to the north at top speed. By that time the seas were rising and the German ships had to reduce speed because the seas breaking over the bows made it impossible to use their forward batteries. The Russians were soon out of sight, and the Germans returned to their patrol lines.

Though the Russians fled when they encountered the German ships, their presence outside the Gulf of Finland sent shock waves through Prince Heinrich's command. The Germans assumed that the Russians were preparing to make Libau a major naval base from which to go on the offensive, with British help. Though the Germans did not know it at the time, however, the Russians had evacuated Libau in the weeks preceding the war. They burned the coal supplies, destroyed the docks, and sank five block ships in the entrances. Though Libau retained limited facilities for a few destroyers, it had effectively ceased to be a naval base, and the odd presence of two Russian cruisers and three large destroyers outside the Gulf of Finland was not going to change that.

But the Germans' worries continued when two British submarines, *E-1* under Lieutenant Commander Noel F. Laurence, RN, and *E-9* under Lieutenant Commander Max K. Horton, RN, entered the Baltic on 17 and 18 October. The two British boats had orders to attack German fleet units and then to go to Libau when their fuel ran low. Surprisingly, the British were also unaware that the Russian navy had already abandoned the port.

The sudden discovery that British submarines were operating in the Baltic alarmed German naval headquarters, and a report received on 21 October indicating that the British boats were based in Libau heightened the apprehension. That report was false, but it was based on a correct report that *E-1* had entered the nearly abandoned harbor on 21 October. What the report did not say was that *E-1* left very soon afterward.[11]

Still unaware that the Russian navy had pulled out of Libau and that the British submarine *E-1* was now in Revel, the Germans started getting ready to attack Libau. In the meantime, Kontreadmiral Behring was preparing to make his third attempt to lure the Russians out of the Gulf of Finland and into waters where his combined force of light cruisers, torpedo boats, and U-boats could attack them.

On the recommendation of Kapitänleutnant Hermann Gercke, an officer on Prince Heinrich's staff, Behring drew two airplanes and their crews from the Putzig naval air station, and on 24 October 1914 von Gorrissen, Killinger, von Tempsky, and Schwarz, together with their Rumpler 4Bs, were hoisted on board the light cruiser SMS *Friedrich Carl*. In addition to having them spot mines and search for British submarines, Kontreadmiral Behring planned to send the Rumplers into the Gulf of Finland as far as Helsingfors and Revel to learn the movements of the Russian fleet.

Initially, the plan was to station three U-boats—*U-23*, *U-25*, and *U-26*—at seven-mile intervals on a line at the entrance to the Gulf of Finland, supported by three light cruisers and half a flotilla of torpedo boats. At the same time, a smaller force made up of the five school cruisers under Kontreadmiral Jasper would demonstrate in the entrance to the Bay of Riga. Kontreadmiral Behring hoped that Jasper's movements would draw the Russian warships out of the gulf and across the U-boat line, where they could be torpedoed and the German cruisers and torpedo boats could engage them. Behring intended to send both Rumplers into the Gulf of Finland to report on the advance and strength of the Russian force that would be responding to Jasper's demonstration.

It was a good plan, but it didn't work. The weather was so bad for most of the week-long operation that the Rumplers could not fly, and at the midpoint of the operation Prince Heinrich's headquarters ordered Behring to send immediately a large part of his force to Memel, where a "Russian occupation . . . was probable." Should the Russians take Memel, they would have a strong base for submarines and torpedo boats. Along with Behring's force Prince Heinrich sent five block ships to close the harbor at Memel.

The instant loss of about half his strength was a setback for Kontreadmiral Behring and a disappointment for the Rumpler aircrews, who had yet to fly a mission. Behring still had three cruisers, the U-boats, and two Rumplers, but without his torpedo boat screen he was unwilling to run the risk of being torpedoed while the *Friedrich Carl* stopped to set the airplanes on the water or recover them after their mission. Then, at 9:17 a.m. on 29 October, he received another message from Prince Heinrich's headquarters that the British submarines *E-1* and *E-9* were in Libau. Behring was "to break off his operations and immediately proceed with his entire force to Libau" where he was to blockade and shell the port.

By this time Killinger was starting to believe that he was no closer to seeing action than he had been on the *Berlin*. When he learned of the new orders his spirits rose because he knew that the Rumplers would be needed to make reconnaissance flights over the town and direct shell fire. Here at last was his chance to see combat—unless something else went wrong.

When the *Friedrich Carl* arrived off Libau a Baltic storm was blowing and the seas were very high, precluding any attempt to set the planes in the water. In any case, visibility was so low that even if they had gotten airborne, they would have been useless. But it was not just the weather that dashed Killinger's hopes for action. Kontreadmiral Behring had suspected that the British submarines would be gone by the time his force arrived off Libau, and he was right. *E-1* had left the port a week earlier, and *E-9* had never been there. Even if the submarines had been present, Behring lacked the resources to properly blockade and shell the port. And the submarines posed a far greater threat to Behring's force than his ships did to them. In the meantime, the panic over the Russians taking Memel had evaporated when the local garrison commander told his "rescuers" that there had been no threat to Memel.

On 30 October the *Friedrich Carl* entered Neufahrwasser, the naval base at Danzig, her arrival there marking the end of Kontreadmiral

Behring's third attempt to engage the Russians. Behring returned the two airplanes and their crews to Putzig, noting that though the planes had not been used, they had withstood the stormy weather while strapped to the deck, protected by the ship's superstructure. He also noted that the planes' presence had in no way interfered with the ship's ability to fight. The admiral's observation would influence the unfolding drama of Killinger's wartime experience.

As Killinger and von Gorrissen were leaving the ship to return to Putzig for more training, the *Friedrich Carl* was already preparing to lead an attack on Libau that would include the five block ships previously intended for use at Memel. That same attack would feature a ship of a different sort that would play a large role in the naval careers of Killinger and von Gorrissen: the former British coal freighter SS *Glyndwr*.

The *Glyndwr*'s owners, the Scarisbrick Steamship Company of Cardiff, had sent the 6,000-ton ship with a load of coal to Danzig on the eve of World War I. She was in Danzig waiting to discharge her cargo when the war started and the German navy seized her. In September the Germans sent the ship and her cargo to Memel to serve as a coaling station. She was still there on 9 November when Kontreadmiral Behring issued orders that she was to be used as a temporary tender and barracks ship for two seaplanes and their crews. The admiral sent Oberleutnant zur See Hellmuth Riensberg to oversee the temporary conversion together with a "small supply of fuel, bombs and spare parts."[12]

When Riensberg reported that the ship was ready, Kontreadmiral Behring sent von Gorrissen and Killinger to Memel with orders to fly reconnaissance missions to Libau. At the same time Behring had two new seaplanes and crews assigned to the *Friedrich Carl* for the raid on Libau.

Following a one-week deployment in Memel with the *Glyndwr*, von Gorrissen and Killinger went with the ship to the imperial shipyard in Danzig, where the *Glyndwr* was to be converted to a fully equipped seaplane tender, the first in the German navy. In addition to receiving two 105-mm guns, the *Glyndwr* was also armed with four 37-mm rapid-fire cannon and four machine guns, and was equipped with four boom cranes to set the planes on the water and recover them. The ship had no below-decks hangars, so the four airplanes were stored on the main deck, two aft of the midship superstructure and two forward. Spare parts, fuel, and bombs were stored in the after cargo hold, and the forward hold was used as aircrew quarters and an engine repair shop.[13]

When she came out of the yard on 15 December 1914, the *Glyndwr* had a crew of four officers and eighty-seven men, plus the four aircrews. She made the short trip across the Gulf of Danzig to the Bay of Putzig, where she anchored and remained until 23 March 1915, training aircrews in overwater reconnaissance and aerial navigation, and developing techniques and procedures for operating seaplanes from a tender with the fleet.

Along with training missions that stressed aerial navigation Killinger and von Gorrissen flew real reconnaissance patrols looking for enemy submarines and newly laid Russian minefields. One of their regular patrol routes took them northwest to Gotland Island and back, a nearly 300-nautical-mile round trip. Another route took them out over the central Baltic to patrol below latitude 56° N. A third route took them northeast to Libau and back, a 280-nautical-mile round trip. While they were training, an event took place that would have a direct impact on Killinger's future.

On 25 January 1915 the Parseval semirigid airship PL-19 lifted off at Königsberg and headed toward Libau, 109 nautical miles to the north. It carried enough fuel for just ten hours and had no radio, apparently to reduce weight and to compensate for its bomb load. Oberleutnant zur See Ernst Meier was in command, and one of the craft's six crewmembers was a volunteer chaplain, Dr. Otto Roetzell. Bad weather had plagued the PL-19 for several days, either preventing it from flying or forcing it to abort the mission and return to Königsberg. The weather on this day was marginal, with gusty winds and snowstorms.[14]

The airship approached Libau from seaward at 9:30 a.m. at a very low altitude—perhaps five hundred feet—and continued across the city until it reached the Rowno Railway, at which point it descended almost to the ground and discharged a cloud of smoke that momentarily hid it from view. The airship rose as the smoke cleared and started back across the city, still at a very low altitude.

As the PL-19 drifted across the city, crewmen hurled bombs from the windows at the ground below. They dropped nine bombs in all, and the engine noise and explosions brought swarms of people into the streets. Air raids were a new phenomenon, and apparently no one thought to take cover. The crewmen were clearly visible in the car, as was the number of the airship painted on the side. Three trucks of the frontier guard came roaring down the road, filled with men firing rifles and machine guns at the airship. The airship turned south toward the sea with the army trucks in hot pursuit and the soldiers keeping up a steady volume of small arms fire.

The Germans in the PL-19 fired back at the soldiers with rifles and at least one machine gun mounted in a window. As the airship crossed the shoreline about twelve miles south of Libau it was seen to be slowly sinking, tail down. About a mile offshore it came to rest with its tail in the water and the nose pointed upward at a steep angle. The exchange of gunfire continued as three armed tugs arrived. The Germans fired at the tugs as they approached, and one of the tugs fired into the wreck with a 37-mm gun. The round ignited a fuel tank, forcing the Germans to leap into the sea. The Russians dragged all seven of them on board the tugs.

The Germans' official report of the mission declared that the PL-19 was flying too low because of the weather conditions and the airship's "heavy" bomb load. The most likely explanation for the ship's very low altitude, however, is that Oberleutnant zur See Meier was flying beneath the cloud cover so that he could see the ground and his target. The Germans also believed that enemy ground fire had seriously damaged the ship by the time it had dropped its bombs, preventing it from climbing to a higher altitude. On that point they were probably right.

About six weeks later, on 16 March 1915, German border police shot and killed a man north of Memel. A note on his body indicated that he was a Russian spy whose task it was to determine if there was a naval presence in Memel, if the harbor was mined, and if it was ice-free. The contents of the note clearly implied that the Russians were planning an attack on Memel from land and sea. In fact, the attack from land was already under way.[15]

The Russians entered the city on 18 March. After heavy fighting that included attack, counterattack, and house-to-house street fighting, the Germans threw them out on 22 March. The Russians retreated north toward Libau, pursued by German infantry, and the Germans sent in their cruisers to shell the Libau-Memel road to disrupt the retreat. The situation created an instant need for aerial reconnaissance and fire control, and on 23 March SMS *Glyndwr* entered a long, narrow lagoon known as Kuriches Haff with four airplanes and their aircrews.

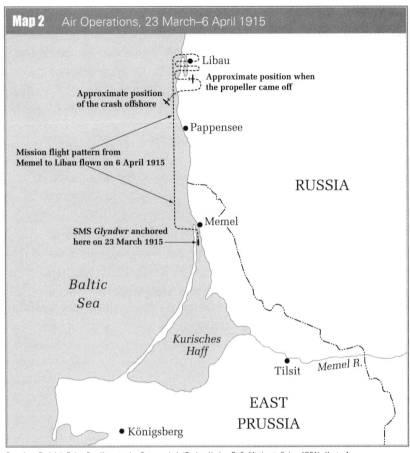

Map 2   Air Operations, 23 March–6 April 1915

Libau

Approximate position when
the propeller came off

Approximate position
of the crash offshore

Pappensee

Mission flight pattern from
Memel to Libau flown on 6 April 1915

RUSSIA

Memel

SMS *Glyndwr* anchored
here on 23 March 1915

*Baltic
Sea*

*Kurisches
Haff*

Tilsit   *Memel R.*

EAST
PRUSSIA

• Königsberg

Based on Rudolph Firle, *Der Krieg in der Ostee*, vol. 1 (Berlin: Verlag E. S. Mittler & Sohn, 1921), Karte 1.

The lagoon is a shallow, nontidal bay that abuts, but is not a part of, the Memel harbor. The sixty-one-mile-long lagoon is fully enclosed by a natural breakwater called the Curonian Spit that runs along the entire west side of the lagoon from a small town called Kranz, near Königsberg, to the Memel Strait. Entry into the lagoon is through the Memel Strait. Though the Kuriches Haff was generally too shallow for the *Glyndwr's* nineteen-foot draft, the water just inside the spit and across the front of the city and harbor was deep enough to accommodate the ship. The natural breakwater provided excellent surface conditions for takeoffs and landings, and Libau was just forty-nine nautical miles north—less than an hour away.

Though the harbor conditions were excellent, the weather remained ugly. Nevertheless, Erich Killinger and his fellow aviators finally got to see some action. In addition to reconnaissance flights between Memel and Libau they flew patrols out to sea to prevent the Russians from sending an unannounced naval force to Memel. They flew daily in the bad weather, prompting Kontreadmiral Behring to laud his airmen in his final report:

> Our expectations for our airmen were not disappointed. Even when the thermometer was well below zero, the machines were set out on, and recovered from, the water. Despite cloud cover and snow flurries the airmen flew and remained aloft at great altitude for long periods. Each day at dawn a machine flew a mission northwest and returned along the coast to observe enemy troop movements. On one occasion Oberbootsmannsmaat Bachmann and Fähnrich zur See Günther Schwarz made a forty-kilometer inland flight, and despite ground fire and the danger of the engine being hit, made a low-level reconnaissance of the back-country and returned with valuable information. They made almost daily flights over Libau to see if the fortress works had been expanded and to determine if the harbor was again usable. They reported that the condition of the harbor remained unchanged and there were very few soldiers present, but they always received ground fire. The harbor entrances were impassable for medium-size ships, and the harbor was almost fully choked with ice.[16]

On 28 March, von Gorrissen and Killinger took off on patrol at 6 a.m. and headed north up the coast toward Libau. They flew at five thousand feet, looking down through broken cloud cover as they approached the mole, or breakwater, at the harbor's south entrance. Though the visibility was poor, Killinger saw what appeared to be a submarine near the outer mole at the harbor entrance.[17]

He leaned forward, rapped von Gorrissen on the back of his head to get his attention, and pointed down. Von Gorrissen looked over the side of his cockpit, saw the submarine, and banked into a hard left turn. Killinger tried to keep his eyes on the submarine, but the heavy cloud cover made it impossible. After flying past the spot where they had seen the submarine, von Gorrissen dropped down to get below the cloud cover and leveled off at about a thousand feet. The submarine was still there, and von Gorrissen lined up to make a bomb run. Killinger leaned as far out over the left side of the fuselage as he could, trying to judge when to release the bombs. When he judged that the airplane was in the right spot he pulled the release handle, dropping the ten bombs beneath the lower wings, and von Gorrissen hauled back on the stick.

As soon as the bombs fell away, the Rumpler entered the cloud cover. Neither von Gorrissen nor Killinger saw where the bombs landed, but both were sure they had scored a direct hit. Von Gorrissen circled back and passed over the spot where he thought the submarine should have been. They could see the mole through the broken cloud cover, but there was no sign of the submarine. Elated to have actually sunk a submarine, they headed back toward Memel.

After landing, Killinger submitted a report and a sketch of the mole where they had seen the submarine to Fregattenkapitän Franz Halm, the captain of SMS *Lübeck*. At noon, the *Lübeck* and two torpedo boats, SMS *G-134* and SMS *G-135*, left Memel and headed toward Libau to look for the submarine while von Gorrissen and Killinger took off to search the area off the Libau entrance and direct the surface vessels to the spot. After von Gorrissen and Killinger left, the *Glyndwr* upped anchor and steamed to Pappensee, twenty-eight nautical miles north of Memel and twenty-one nautical miles south of Libau.

The three surface ships found no trace of the submarine, and there seems to have been some confusion as to what the two aviators had really seen and bombed. The two torpedo boat captains, Kapitänleutnant Fritz Rebensburg and Kapitänleutnant Heinz Menche, said that the nature of the mole's construction made it impossible to secure a submarine alongside, and they believed that the airmen had confused a sunken scow off the mole for a submarine.

In their after-action report, von Gorrissen and Killinger never said that the boat was tied alongside the mole; nor did they say that it was submerged when they attacked it. They did not say that the boat was on the surface, either, though that is the implication. The question is, did they actually see a submarine? No one knows for sure, but one thing is certain—they bombed something.

Despite high winds and rough seas off Pappensee, Killinger and von Gorrissen were able to land on the water and recover on board the *Glyndwr*. All the vessels and aircraft that had been involved in the search were safely back in Memel at 8 p.m. It had been a good day for von Gorrissen and Killinger, and both men felt that they had finally gotten into the war.

CAPTURED

6 April 1915

Tuesday, 6 April 1915, dawned clear and cold, and the surface of the water inside the Kuriches Haff was like glass. On the *Glyndwr*, Von Gorrissen and Killinger, bundled in their heavy flight suits, inspected their Rumpler while the deck crew prepared to set it on the water. While von Gorrissen walked around the plane examining the control surfaces and looking for oil leaks, Killinger made sure the 10-pound bombs hanging from the lower wings were firmly locked into their racks.

Their airplane was showing signs of wear from heavy use, particularly the engine. The most noticeable performance change was the plane's inability to climb above four thousand feet, but there were other indications that the engine needed a major overhaul or replacement. Oil consumption was greater than normal, and there was a faint knock when von Gorrissen applied full power. Von Gorrissen nevertheless considered the *Flugzeug-51* to be reliable because the engine ran smoothly and started without difficulty. He did not know that aircraft's biggest problem was not *in* the engine.

Satisfied that the plane was ready to go, the two aviators climbed into their cockpits and a ground crewman stepped up to spin the propeller. Von Gorrissen checked that all switches were off, noting that the throttle was against its Off stop, and extended his left arm straight up with his fist clenched. The ground crewman saw the signal and pulled the propeller through the three half-revolutions required to clear the cylinders.

Killinger stowed his maps, checked that the flare pistol and flares were in their racks, and made sure the bomb release lever was locked. His final act before the *Flugzeug-51* was lifted off the deck was to examine the hoisting hook. Satisfied that all was in order, Killinger leaned forward and tapped von Gorrissen twice on the head, signaling that the plane was ready to be set on the water, and then sat down and buckled in.

Von Gorrissen nodded that he understood and leaned forward slightly to prime the cylinders with a hand pump. He flipped the ignition switch and advanced the throttle to fast idle, then looked around to be sure the deck was clear of people before extending his left arm straight up with his fist balled and the index finger pointing straight up. The ground crewman spun the propeller, and the engine coughed three times and fired up in a steady roar. Von Gorrissen pulled the throttle back to idle and signaled the deck officer that they were ready to be set on the water.

As the *Flugzeug-51* settled onto the water, the hoisting cable slackened and Killinger stood up and released the hook. He raised both arms and brought them down until they were horizontal and fully stretched, the signal to the deck officer that the plane was free and ready to fly. The lift operator pulled up the hook as von Gorrissen advanced the throttle and started to taxi away from the ship.

The *Glyndwr*'s sailors lined the rail and waved their hats as the *Flugzeug-51* started its takeoff run. Killinger waved back, then faced forward and scrunched down in the rear cockpit. The Rumpler lifted off easily, water streaming from its pontoons. Von Gorrissen took the aircraft up to three thousand feet, banked left, and headed out over the Baltic.[1] Twenty miles out he turned northeast toward Libau, searching for Russian navy units moving south and for the British submarines that were believed to be operating in the Baltic. When they arrived at Libau they were to fly over the harbor and city looking for any signs of naval or military activity, and bomb any military target they saw. Visibility was unlimited, the air was clear and bitingly cold, and the sea below was empty.

When the *Flugzeug-51* came abeam of Libau two hours later, von Gorrissen banked right to come in across the harbor, approaching the coast over the huge ice fields lying across the harbor entrance. The Russian navy sank five block ships in the harbor entrance after withdrawing from Libau, and Killinger could clearly see the five hulks, which at low water were partially exposed. Apparently he was unaware that the wrecks were block ships, because he later attributed their sinking to either the cruiser SMS *Magdeburg*, which had shelled Libau on 2 August 1914, or to the 28 March attack by the *Lübeck* together with the torpedo boats *G-134* and *G-135*.[2]

On nearing Libau, von Gorrissen started gaining altitude. The plane climbed sluggishly and the faint knocking noise grew a little louder, but von Gorrissen had grown accustomed to that and ignored it. He made a mental note that their 100-pound bomb load was too heavy for the aging airplane. The airplane's inability to climb beyond four thousand feet did not worry him, because at that time no Russian fighters were operating near Libau and the city's antiaircraft defenses consisted entirely of rifles and machine guns.[3] At four thousand feet they would be effectively out of range for the Russians' small arms fire, and he could always change direction if things became too hot. They flew across the harbor and the city, looking down on the Russians.

Thirty minutes later, having seen all they had come to see and finding nothing unusual, they turned south, continuing to fly over land until they were south of Libau. They were a few miles south of the city when the *Flugzeug-51*'s major problem made itself known. The faint knocking noise that von Gorrissen had grown accustomed to hearing ended with a loud bang that anyone who has ever snapped an axle would recognize. The propeller spun off to the right, slicing through the right float as it went. Propeller pilots have an old saying that "you don't know how hot the day is until the fan stops turning." It was bitterly cold at three thousand feet, but von Gorrissen and Killinger had good reason to start sweating as von Gorrissen started looking for a place to crash-land.

He had only two choices, and neither was attractive. He could come down on land, preferably on the beach, or he could glide out to sea and make a single-float water landing. The first choice was particularly unappealing because even if they survived the crash, which was unlikely, the Russians would capture them almost immediately. But going down at sea was not a very attractive option either. With only one float there was an absolute certainty that they were going to end up in the near-freezing water, and their chances of surviving for more than a short time were zero. Faced with two poor choices, von Gorrissen chose to glide out to sea because he felt that their chances of surviving the crash were much better than on land. And a German patrol boat or fishing boat might come along and rescue them before they died of hypothermia or the Russians got them. While he still had altitude von Gorrissen had Killinger jettison their bomb load. The bombs fell away and exploded harmlessly in the water.

While the *Flugzeug-51* was gliding down toward the water, Killinger destroyed his charts and signal book. He shoved a flare pistol into his coat pocket and strapped a signal flares cartridge belt around his waist, thinking that the flares might come in handy. As the plane settled toward the water he climbed out onto the left float, intending to use his weight to slow the airplane's inevitable roll to the right as the smashed float filled. The idea seemed sound in the cockpit, but in application it was a flop. Meanwhile, in the front cockpit, von Gorrissen was unbuckling so that he could get out quickly if the plane hit and turned turtle. It was another idea that seemed good at the moment.

When the *Flugzeug-51* touched down, about a mile offshore and five miles south of Libau, the ruptured float became a very effective brake that whipped the Rumpler around to the right and to an abrupt halt, hurling Killinger off the good float. Von Gorrissen was catapulted headlong from the cockpit and hit the leading edge of the left wing before he landed in the water and sank out of sight. Moments after von Gorrissen hit the water, Killinger popped to the surface, coughing and gasping for air. Looking about quickly, he saw the wreck heeled over but still afloat, and swam toward it. His strength was nearly gone by the time he reached the wrecked plane, and it was only with great difficulty that he managed to pull himself out of the icy water. Von Gorrissen had also surfaced and made for the wreck but was almost unconscious when he reached the good float. Killinger literally clawed him out of the water and dragged him onto the float.

The two huddled together on the good float, wet to the skin and freezing, but at least out of the water. They were so cold that it took a strenuous effort even to speak to each other. They figured that the wreck would float for two or three hours, during which time "something had to happen." Both men knew that the *Glyndwr*'s crew would become concerned when the *Flugzeug-51* failed to return on time, but could they survive until rescuers arrived? In the distance was a large ice floe, but it was too far away to swim to, and as Killinger later observed, "Lacking the skill of Eskimos we couldn't have survived on the ice anyway."[4]

While they sat and waited, the plane was slowly sinking. As it rolled farther to the right, their perch on the float became increasingly perilous, a situation made worse by their stiff, numb hands. They lost track of time. After what Killinger judged to be about three hours, his hopes started to rise. According to their original estimate, the plane should have sunk by now. They judged that the current and the wind were carrying them southward, toward Memel, and they became confident that the plane would remain afloat for at least another two hours. In fact, they probably had been adrift for no longer than an hour, but they did have reason for hope.

Forty-nine miles south, in Memel, the Germans had already become worried about the *Flugzeug-51*, and at noon on 6 April 1915 the *Lübeck* received word that the plane was overdue and presumed down. The captain immediately ordered the Neufahrwasser auxiliary minesweeping division to break off work and proceed north in line abreast to search for the missing airplane. The *Lübeck* and the *Glyndwr* also started north, searching farther out to sea.[5]

Meanwhile, von Gorrissen and Killinger were watching a rowboat approaching from land. The immediate question was, "friend or foe?" Given that they had crashed very near Libau, it was a silly question. But von Gorrissen expressed the optimistic opinion that the Russians had no rowboats along the coast, and the two downed airmen happily concluded that the boat belonged to German fishermen. Their optimism remained undiminished until the people in the boat fired at them. Von Gorrissen, still clinging to the delusion that the men in the boat were Germans, concluded, "Obviously they think we're Russians," and on that happy thought they began waving.[6]

The salvo of rifle fire that followed instantly dispelled their optimism, and they stopped waving. The men in the boat were clearly not Germans. Whoever they were, they were poor shots. The rounds were passing overhead and striking the water around them, but none hit either man or the airplane. The poor shooting was probably due to the unsteady platform from which the riflemen were firing. As the boat pulled nearer, Killinger and von Gorrissen made out two riflemen standing in the boat; both were Russian soldiers. Their optimism vanished entirely.

When the boat was one hundred yards away, one of the soldiers shouted, "Russki? Prusski?" Apparently they had not yet determined whether they were shooting at fellow Russians or at hated Prussians. Regardless, it was clear that the Russians had a "shoot first and ask questions later" policy. Killinger shouted back, "Nix Russki! Nix Prusski!" He was not trying to mislead the Russians by claiming that they were neither Russian nor Prussian. He was being honest. He and von Gorrissen were from Baden, not Prussia.

The response obviously puzzled the two soldiers, who talked animatedly to each other. They seemed to conclude that if the two men on the airplane were not Russians or Prussians, they must be Austrians, and they opened fire again. They continued to shoot ineffectively as the boat pulled closer to the plane. When the boat was virtually within bayonet range, the Russians stopped firing and motioned the two Germans to get into the water and swim to the boat. Having no choice in the matter, Killinger and von Gorrissen complied and were soon pulled into the rowboat.

Shortly before dark on 6 April, one of the trawlers that had been sent north to search for the missing *Flugzeug-51* spotted the wrecked airplane, still afloat, not far from Pappensee, about seventeen nautical miles from where it had gone down. The trawler went alongside the wreck and hoisted it on board, but there was no sign of the crew.[7]

THE FIRST ESCAPE ATTEMPT

6–16 April 1915

Killinger and von Gorrissen found their situation only marginally improved in the rowboat. Although they were no longer in immediate danger, they were drenched and exhausted. While the civilian oarsmen the two soldiers had pressed into service controlled the boat, the soldiers searched their prisoners for weapons and valuables. They found Killinger's flare pistol and flares, and the young German held his breath when one of the soldiers seemed to be about to shoot him. The moment passed as the boat's crew became more interested in distributing the flares they took from him.[1]

The two soldiers made no more threatening gestures, but they kept their attention focused on the two Germans as the civilians took up their oars and started the hour-long pull back to shore. The wind had freshened, and the two soaked airmen shivered in misery. Making the situation even more uncomfortable, the Russians made the prisoners sit with their hands atop their heads during the entire trip to shore.

A large group of Russian soldiers was waiting on the beach when the boat landed. Badly fatigued, their legs stiff from cold, Killinger and von Gorrissen were unable to move when the Russians ordered them out of the boat. Taking the Germans' inability to move for refusal, several soldiers dragged them out, bound their hands and feet, blindfolded them, and threw them like sacks into the back of a horse-drawn cart. Killinger and von Gorrissen were too exhausted to care. It was now about 8 p.m. on 6 April.

An hour later the cart stopped in front of a well-constructed house. Soldiers dragged the two Germans from the cart, removed their blindfolds and freed their hands and legs, and pushed them through the door. A large fire in an open fireplace warmed the room, and the men could feel life returning to their hands and feet.

They discovered that they were in the personal quarters of the local garrison commander, who entered the room and looked them over. The Russian officer directed an orderly to bring the prisoners hot tea and bread, and indicated with gestures that they should strip off their wet clothing. While they were undressing, another orderly entered the room with towels and blankets, followed by another carrying wood that he added to the already blazing fire. The officer said something in Russian, and the orderlies quickly pushed two large chairs in front of the fireplace. The officer motioned the Germans to sit.

Seated in oversized chairs and warmed by hot tea, bread, and warm blankets, the two airmen thawed quickly. In their ignorance they assumed that this was the treatment that they, as officers, could expect. In fact, the Germans were about to experience an interrogation technique that all World War I belligerents employed. They were comfortably settled, enjoying the hospitality of the garrison commander's house, and starting to nod off when the interpreter arrived.

From the way he was dressed, the two Germans assumed the interpreter was a civilian, probably a schoolteacher whom the garrison commander had pressed into service as an interpreter for this occasion. His excellent German impressed them, and they felt reassured when he told them that he had lived in Germany before the war. The man seemed helpful and, though he was a Russian, showed no sign of animosity. He was deferential, especially toward von Gorrissen, either because von Gorrissen was senior in rank or because of his aristocratic name.

The "interpreter" engaged them in a general conversation about their welfare, where they were from in Germany, and the tragedy of the war. He wondered if they believed in a Russian or German victory, and concluded that it probably did not matter because the war would certainly be settled by a negotiated peace. In the course of the generalities he touched on military matters and gradually came to the matter that interested him the most. Were they the aviators who had bombed the train station?

There was no sign of anger or accusation in his voice; he simply wanted to know. But Killinger and von Gorrissen knew instantly that they were in danger. They had not bombed anything except a patch of open water, but how were they to convince the Russians of that? They knew of no other airplane that had flown over Libau that day. They were fortunate that their airplane had crashed into the sea south of Libau. Had the Russians recovered the wreck, they would have found the bomb racks empty and would have drawn the logical conclusion.

Killinger and von Gorrissen failed to recognize that the Russian had not said *when* the train station was bombed, and both assumed that it must have happened on the same day they flew over the city. The PL-19 had flown over the city in January and had dropped bombs, and German army airplanes had also flown over the city since, and some of them had dropped bombs. Von Gorrissen told the Russian that they had dropped their bombs before they crashed at sea rather than saying that they had dropped their bombs *into* the sea before they crashed. His vague answer left open the possibility that they had dropped their bombs on the train station and *then* crashed at sea, and it would come to haunt the two Germans.

The interpreter remained suspicious, but he could not be sure, and after asking a few more questions and receiving evasive answers he left. When he was gone and there was no one left in the room who understood German, Killinger and von Gorrissen put their heads together to work out a common story to be used during all subsequent questioning. Killinger also brought up the matter of escaping.

He correctly estimated that they were near Pappensee, about twenty miles north of the German border and the Russian town of Polangen. He knew from observations made during previous missions to the south that the road from Libau to Polangen was heavily forested on both sides. The road would be their guide, he explained to von Gorrissen, and the forests would offer them cover.

The best time for a prisoner to escape is while still in the hands of frontline troops or, as in this case, garrison troops. Typically the soldiers who guard recently taken prisoners are not accustomed to handling them; and indeed, these guards carelessly left the two German prisoners alone in the room. Further, Killinger and von Gorrissen were closer to their own lines than they were likely to be at any time again during their captivity. But in this case Killinger was overly optimistic. The country between Pappensee and the border was teeming with Russian soldiers, and the two Germans were in no shape to make the run. They were badly fatigued, had no food, and their clothes were still soaking wet. Even the optimistic Killinger recognized that "wearing our wet clothes in that extreme cold would have made it impossible for us to have walked more than a few hundred meters."

But before they were able to put their hastily conceived plan into effect, the comfortable interlude in the Russian officer's house came to an abrupt end. Several guards entered the room and, using gestures, ordered them to put on their uniforms and go outside. They were again bound and blindfolded and tossed into the cart. For about two hours they jolted through the night until the cart stopped at a shack that appeared to be in the middle of nowhere.

The guards pulled them from the cart, untied them, and hustled them into a situation very different from the comfortable garrison commander's house. The shack was a resting place for local troops and was crowded with soldiers, many of whom were drunk. There was a fire in a large stone fireplace and several long tables that were littered with dirty tin plates and open bottles, apparently vodka. It was a dangerous situation, but at least the room was warm.

They moved as close to the fire as they could, trying to soak up as much heat as possible. They knew that this was just a temporary stop for their guards to get something to eat and drink. Nothing was offered to the prisoners. Standing by the fire, they concluded that none of the soldiers spoke or understood German, which, coupled with the fact that no one was paying any attention to them, gave them an opportunity to talk openly.

Killinger brought up escape and put forward a second escape plan. He suggested that when the opportunity arose, they grab a rifle, kill their guards, and run out of the hut before the drunken soldiers could react. Then they would make their way to the coast and follow the coastline south to the border. He figured that the ice along the shore would offer the advantage of hiding their tracks.

It was a poor plan that offered no hope for success, and von Gorrissen rejected it. He pointed out that they were badly outnumbered in the shack, and drunk or not, the Russians would have no trouble killing them. Even if they did get away and into cover, they were wet, weak from exposure, and in no condition to reach the border in freezing weather. Von Gorrissen's factual appraisal of the situation and seniority in rank forced Killinger to drop the matter.

Disappointed but not discouraged, Killinger formulated a plan on his own to be put into effect when they were under way and an opportunity presented itself. The new plan was basically the same as the plan he had come up with in the shack—somehow overpower the guards and escape. He assumed that he and von Gorrissen would be in the same wagon and could coordinate their attack. That did not happen.

Two surly soldiers carrying lengths of telephone wire came for them and roughly shoved them outside. They bound the prisoners' hands behind their backs and bound their feet; then they put them in separate wagons, each with a driver accompanied by two soldiers. One soldier walked at the rear of the wagon and the other sat in the wagon watching the prisoner. Both soldiers were armed with rifles and fixed bayonets. Leading the caravan were three soldiers on horseback; another mounted soldier brought up the rear.

The wire bindings were not very tight, and Killinger soon freed himself, although he remained motionless on the floor of the cart and kept his hands hidden. He was stretched out along the right side of the cart with his feet against the gate. The guard in the cart was sitting in the left front corner, facing aft. His high winter coat collar was turned up, his cap was pulled down over his eyes, and his hands were shoved deep into his coat pockets. The man appeared to be sleeping, and his rifle lay on the wagon floor beside him, within Killinger's reach. The driver, bundled in a heavy coat and a blanket, was bent slightly forward, looking straight ahead. The guard walking at the rear of the wagon was carrying his rifle at sling arms, his hands deep in his pockets, shuffling along with his eyes on the ground.

Killinger knew this was the time to move. But what about von Gorrissen in the next wagon? Since they had not discussed this escape plan, Killinger had no reason to believe that von Gorrissen had freed himself, and he could not call out to von Gorrissen without warning the guards. Somehow he had to alert von Gorrissen because he would not make the break without him. His hastily conceived plan appeared to have already failed when chance intervened.

It was snowing and the night was pitch black, and the driver, who was probably asleep, drove off the road. One wheel sank into a ditch, and the wagon rolled over on its side. As soon as the wagon started to roll, Killinger grabbed the soldier next to him, and both men spilled out into the snow, with Killinger on top. The Russian's head hit something hard, stunning him, and Killinger leaped up, shouting to von Gorrissen to run. The foot guard, alerted by the shouts, lunged at him with his bayonet, which

Killinger grabbed to deflect the blade, cutting his left hand deeply. The guard's thrust was slightly turned, but the point of the bayonet jabbed Killinger in his upper left chest, inflicting a small but painful wound. The mounted soldiers were quickly on the scene, and the second foot guard smashed his rifle butt into Killinger's shoulder, knocking him down.

The escape attempt was finished. Killinger lay on the ground, his hand and chest wounds bleeding, expecting at any moment to be bayoneted. Instead, he was jerked to his feet and roughly bound again, hands behind his back. This time the guards blindfolded both prisoners. The Russians righted the cart, two soldiers shoved him in, and the caravan started off again. Battered, bleeding, and exhausted, he lay facedown on the floor of the cart and finally lost consciousness. The trip lasted all night and into the morning of 7 April 1915.

The caravan arrived in Libau sometime before 9 a.m. and went directly to the train station. The soldiers dragged the prisoners from the cart, freed their hands and feet, and removed the blindfolds. The two young Germans found themselves face-to-face with an angry crowd that was demanding their heads. At that moment, he and von Gorrissen genuinely believed that the mob was going to lynch them. The crowd surged forward, but the guards held them back and hustled the prisoners through the station and onto a platform where a train was waiting. They turned their prisoners over to another guard unit, who shoved the Germans into a fourth-class railcar. Seated on a rough, backless bench, Killinger surveyed his surroundings. Other than their guards, he and von Gorrissen were the only people in the car.

The new guards consisted of a police lieutenant, two police officers, and eight soldiers. The soldiers were divided into two groups, with four at each end of the car. The three policemen sat together on a bench at the front of the car. Killinger examined the window next to him and found that it was nailed closed. He was not yet experienced enough to realize it, but he and von Gorrissen were now in the custody of men who knew how to handle prisoners.

Shortly before the train pulled out of the station a Russian officer came on board and gave each prisoner a clean shirt and underclothes. That proved to be the last kindness they received while they were in Russia. The officer told them that they were being sent to St. Petersburg and would arrive in five days' time. The travel time seemed excessive to Killinger, who knew that St. Petersburg was only about 450 miles northeast of Libau. In his mind he calculated that if the trip took five days, the train would crawl toward its destination at around three miles per hour.

Shortly after the train got under way, the police lieutenant told the two Germans that they were criminals who had murdered innocent women and children, and they would be hanged. He then ordered them to strip. The soldiers searched their clothing and took their personal possessions: money, rings, and Killinger's Penkala pencil. When the search was completed the lieutenant told them to get dressed. Nothing more was said during the trip about their pending execution.

Shortly after they had been thoroughly searched, Killinger discovered why the trip to St. Petersburg was going to take longer than it should have. Instead of going northeast to St. Petersburg, the first leg of the trip took them on a 238-mile detour southeast to Vilna, where they arrived 48 hours later. In Vilna the prisoners were ordered out of the car and were marched through town to a POW camp that held several hundred German enlisted men and one German officer. Believing that the Russians were going to execute them, Killinger and von Gorrissen gave the German officer their home addresses so that he could notify their next of kin about what had happened to them.

The next morning the guards marched them back through the town to the garrison commander's headquarters. There they were separated and questioned individually for two hours. A Russian navy officer questioned Killinger. The man showed no interest in military matters, focusing instead on the bombing attack on the Libau train station. After several minutes of asking questions and making accusations about the train station bombing, the Russian abruptly told him that he would be hanged for that crime.

Killinger had now been told twice that he was to be hanged, and he decided it was time to demand his rights as an officer. Including von Gorrissen in his demands, he complained about the way the Russians had treated them since their capture. He specifically cited being bound and blindfolded, being tossed into a cart like baggage, and being forced to wear wet clothes in subfreezing weather. The Russian answered Killinger's complaints by suggesting that better treatment was available if he cooperated.

The Russian finally dropped the train station bombing and asked questions about U-boats and aircraft, which Killinger later claimed he did not answer. The Russian also wanted to know how much the Germans knew about Russian plans and whether or not the Germans believed that Germany would win the war. Killinger told the Russian that he was too junior in rank to be privy to what the German command was thinking and did not know anything about Russian plans. But he did express confidence that Germany would win the war.

Then the Russian asked a question that revealed how little the Russians actually knew about the German forces. The Russian showed great interest in the whereabouts and movements of the *Friedrich Carl*, obviously unaware that the cruiser hit a mine on 17 November 1914 off Memel and sank. Killinger told him the ship was still operating in the Memel area.

The next question indicated that the Russians were not really convinced that von Gorrissen and Killinger had bombed the train station. The Russian wanted to know about the light cruiser SMS *Augsburg*, which he said had shelled the city, killing several civilians. Killinger knew that the *Augsburg* and *Magdeburg* had shelled the Libau harbor on the evening of 2 August 1914, but he had not been in Memel when it happened; he only had heard about it.

The Russian also wanted to know about a second shelling that had occurred on 28 March 1915, just nine days before Killinger was captured. On that date the *Lübeck*, together with the torpedo boats *G-134* and *G-135*, had shelled Libau in the late afternoon. It suddenly occurred to Killinger that the Russian was unsure exactly when the damage had been done to the train station and whether it was the result of an offshore bombardment or bombs dropped from an airplane.

At the end of the two-hour interrogation, the navy officer turned the prisoners over to the guards, who marched them back to the train station. Killinger and von Gorrissen again boarded a fourth-class car for the remaining five-day trip to St. Petersburg, arriving on 15 April 1915.

Killinger had always wanted to visit St. Petersburg, but this was certainly not the trip he had in mind. Despite the circumstances, though, the sights and sounds in the train station intrigued him: "There was an enormous throng of officers and soldiers on the platform," he later wrote. "There were greasy mystics whose long hair had not been washed since their consecration, as well as English, Japanese, and French officers in pompous dress uniforms, which created a colorful display on the crowded platform. The big Cossacks who were the station guards made a particularly good impression."

As they made their way down the crowded platform, the police lieutenant displayed them to the crowd and behaved as though he had person-
ally captured two dangerous Germans whom he was taking to the Peter
and Paul Fortress. Russian officers who were among the crowd embraced
the police lieutenant as though he was a hero, and the civilians shouted
their approval to the police officer and threats to the Germans.

Outside the train station the guards and prisoners boarded a streetcar
full of civilians. The ride through the city gave Killinger cause to worry
about which way the war was going. The houses were draped with flags,
apparently in celebration of a Russian victory, and the civilians seemed
to be in a festive mood. Not knowing who was actually winning troubled
him, and his circumstances allowed him to think the worst. If the Russians
had won a major victory, though, the war might end soon, and he would be
returning to Germany in the near future. His happy thoughts of an early
release were interrupted when the streetcar stopped at its end station across
the street from the foot of the Kronverkskiy Bridge, which joined the north
bank of the Neva River to Zayachy Island and the Peter and Paul Fortress.

The fortress occupied the entire island and had seen many uses since
its completion in 1740, including housing city offices and serving as the
barracks for the city garrison. The infamous Trubetskoy Bastion Prison
was there as well, a maximum-security facility consisting of sixty-nine
solitary and two punishment cells. The fact that the Russians had brought
them here, to a place reserved for high-profile political prisoners, was not
a good sign.

The police lieutenant, three guards, and both prisoners got off the
streetcar and marched across the bridge, turning left as they stepped onto
Zayachy Island. They walked along the north curtain wall of the fortress to a
heavy gate, entered the fortress, and turned immediately right. The narrow
path in front of them led to the southwest bastion that was the Trubetskoy
Bastion Prison. The six men walked down the path to a heavily guarded
steel door. A Russian officer stepped forward as the police and their prisoners approached. There was an exchange of salutes, and the police lieutenant handed the officer a leather purse and a set of orders. The guard
officer read the orders and asked something about the purse. Then the two
men saluted and the police lieutenant and his subordinates turned and left.

As the policemen walked away, the officer shouted an order and the
heavy doors swung open, allowing the two prisoners and their new guards

to enter the massive stone building. The guard officer led the procession down a passageway, through ten heavy iron doors, and into a long, narrow room that Killinger described as a "dungeon" but was really a long cell block. Looking around at the windowless walls and down the long corridor lined with identical iron doors on both sides, Killinger's heart sank to his feet.

A short distance down the corridor a guard was opening two of the iron cell doors. While the guard methodically went through the unlocking procedure, the officer of the guard suddenly became friendly and spoke to the two prisoners in German. He gave von Gorrissen twenty-two kopeks, which he said the police lieutenant had given him with instructions that the money was to be divided equally between the two prisoners. The police lieutenant had told him that the money was left over from the amount provided for their subsistence during the trip from Vilna to St. Petersburg. Both von Gorrissen and Killinger wondered what prompted the police lieutenant to turn over the money when he could have kept it for himself.

Killinger's frame of mind up to this point had been reasonably optimistic, and he had avoided the serious depression that afflicted many newly captured POWs. A soldier's psychological and emotional reactions to capture varied with the individual, the circumstances surrounding his capture, and where he was confined. Even nationality might play a major role in how a POW reacted.[2] Some prisoners felt ashamed and worried that their loved ones would judge them to be cowards or suspect that they used capture as a form of desertion. Others felt they had let their comrades down. And some felt that they failed to act in a manly fashion by not resisting to the end and dying a hero's death. Others, probably the majority, saw capture as a matter of fact that occurred in all wars and had more to do with unavoidable circumstances than their own failings. For those men, captivity was onerous mostly because of the physical discomfort and crushing boredom it entailed.

Sailors and airmen were less likely to feel shame or a sense of personal failure for being taken prisoner, because in nearly every case the circumstances that brought about their capture were beyond their control—their ship was sunk or their airplane crashed behind enemy lines. Killinger fit into this latter category with one additional factor: he was determined to escape.

Killinger's resolve stemmed in part from his upbringing in a society that lauded devotion to *Kaiser und Vaterland* and his status as an officer candidate in the Imperial Navy, where devotion to duty was a basic tenet that made escaping a matter of obligation. Such a sense of duty was prevalent among captured officers of all the services as well as among enlisted men. But a sense of duty was not the only motivation for escape. Many prisoners escaped simply because they did not want to remain penned behind barbed wire, a feeling that might have been as strong as duty. Freedom is a strong motivator.[3]

His firm intention to escape and return to duty shielded Killinger from most of the psychological issues that many POWs must deal with, and also underscores his sense of self-confidence. He *would* escape; all he needed was the opportunity. The Trubetskoy Bastion Prison was not a place opportunity often visited, but as Killinger walked down the corridor toward his cell, his determination told him it was just a matter of time.

PRISON

16 April–21 May 1915

K illinger was alone in an utterly dark cell. He had eaten nothing since
before his arrival in St. Petersburg, and his hunger was becoming
severe. He thought of a Sherlock Holmes story that he had read in
his childhood. Holmes had escaped from a similar dungeon cell after he
discovered an entrance to an underground river. He knew that the Peter
and Paul Fortress was on an island in the Neva River, but he also knew
that, unlike the fictional detective, he could not escape from this cell.[1]

Being locked in a pitch-dark cell inside a fortress gives a man a lot to
think about and the time to do the thinking. And Killinger was thinking.
The first thing he asked himself was why the Russians had brought him
here. The answer was both fairly obvious and unpleasant: they were going
to carry out their threat to hang him. He went back over everything that he
had been asked about the alleged bombing of the train station in Libau and
the answers he had given. He concluded that the Russians did not know
who had bombed the train station, but he and von Gorrissen were the only
aviators they had in custody. And that thought was not encouraging.

Whether or not the Russians could find some grounds, no matter how
flimsy, to tie him and von Gorrissen to the railroad station bombing was
really not important; they had the power to hang them both, with or without proper grounds. But ever the optimist, Killinger adopted the attitude
that worrying about something over which he had no control was a waste
of time; he focused his efforts on more immediate problems on which he
could take action, which included being moved to a cell where he could
make contact with other prisoners, and having his wounds attended to.
He also constructed a mental list of less important things, intending to

make demands as soon as the opportunity appeared. It came sooner than he expected.

He did not know what time it was or how long he had been in the cell when he heard footsteps outside the door, followed by the rattle of keys in the locks and the metallic rasping of the iron bolts being withdrawn. The first thing that came to his mind was that they were coming to execute him. Not wanting to show fear, he stood at attention. The light in the cell came on and a Russian officer stepped inside. The absence of guards did not reassure Killinger. The officer was wearing a sidearm and was perfectly capable of herding him out to a gallows.

In flawless German the Russian asked Killinger if he was ready to cooperate. Still at attention, Killinger immediately asked how long he was going to be kept in a dark, solitary cell. The officer shrugged his shoulders and said that depended on Killinger. The interrogations would last until they were finished, and they would be finished only when he had told them all they wanted to know. Angry, Killinger launched into a lengthy complaint about the treatment he had received since his capture. He demanded a light in his cell, meals, and a doctor to treat his cut hand and chest wound, which had become infected. He also demanded the return of his ring, pencil, and money. Without the money he could not buy necessities such as toiletries. And he demanded to see the American consul, who represented German interests in Russia.

In the tone of voice used to deal with an obstreperous child the Russian dismissed his demands, especially the demand for money, saying that Killinger had no grounds for complaint. He had received the treatment due a captured officer, including ample rations on the train, for which the guard commander had paid. When Killinger did not answer, the Russian shrugged again, said that he hoped he would be comfortable in his quarters, and left. The door closed, the bolts rattled into place, and the light went out.

Alone again in the dark Killinger realized why the police lieutenant had given him and von Gorrissen the twenty-two kopeks. It was to hide the fact that the lieutenant had pocketed the rest of the money without buying food for the prisoners. He also mulled the reality that he was a mere Fähnrich zur See, not even a commissioned officer yet, and had little of value to tell the Russians even had he wanted to talk. He seriously considered making up something to satisfy them.

Either his demands had some effect or the Russians decided on an alternate interrogation method. Later that day the light came on in his cell, and for the first time he could closely examine his surroundings. The cell was small, but actually larger than he had imagined from his touch-and-feel inspection in the dark. An iron bed was fastened to the wall, as was a square iron plate that served as a table, on which was a tin wash-basin. The toilet was a wooden bucket. His demands produced two other improvements. A covering over an opening in the wall near the ceiling was removed, allowing some natural light and fresh air into the room. The ceiling was twelve feet above the floor, however, and there was no way he could reach the opening. He was also allowed to exercise outdoors in a small yard for an hour between eleven each morning and noon.

Shortly after the light came on, a Russian orderly entered the cell carrying what looked like a clothing bag in his left hand and told Killinger to undress. Killinger complied, but stopped at his undershorts; the orderly told him to remove them too. Then he reached into the clothing bag and produced a set of baggy undershorts, a pair of black slippers, and a dark blue caftan, the full-length robe that most Russians wore as their outer garment. While Killinger dressed, the orderly gathered Killinger's uniform and shoes and stuffed them into the clothing bag. Without another word, he left. Killinger found the clothes surprisingly comfortable, and they were clean.

Even the meals improved. Considering the circumstances, they were surprisingly good. Three meals a day were shoved through a narrow sliding panel at waist level in the door: a breakfast of tea and bread served at 9 a.m., a meat-and-potato soup at noon, and tea and bread for dinner at 6 p.m. His lunch was accompanied by a fork and spoon, which were taken from him after the meal. He managed to "embezzle" a wooden spoon that soon proved to be particularly useful.

During the first eight days of improved conditions, the Russians allowed Killinger and von Gorrissen to exercise in the yard together every day. The first thing they learned when they were able to speak face-to-face was that they were in adjacent cells. That alone produced a huge morale lift, and when they discovered that the prison's stone walls were excellent sound conductors they devised a "wireless" communication system. Tapping the wall with a wooden spoon produced a higher-pitched sound, while pounding the wall with a fist produced a lower-pitched sound. They communicated in Morse code; a spoon tap was short and a fist thump was long. The only safe opportunities they had to send Morse messages were during the brief periods when the guard left his post to get their meals. The system was slow and relatively ineffective, but it kept them in touch in between their daily meetings in the exercise yard.

The interrogations went on daily, and they were able to keep each other informed about what questions were being asked so that they could give the same answers and avoid contradicting each other. The system worked effectively until the guard discovered what they were doing and moved von Gorrissen to a cell farther away and stopped their daily exercise together in the yard. Even separated they could still communicate by Morse code, but they no longer had an opportunity to discuss matters face-to-face.

The separation and loss of daily contact with von Gorrissen seriously depressed Killinger, who came to believe that death would be his only relief. It was the first time Killinger lost his focus, but his period of depression was short. The way to overcome depression, he decided, was to refocus on improving his lot. He needed a mission and a goal. He knew that he could not let the Russians get him down, and he began demanding to speak with the German-speaking officer. After several requests the officer finally came to his cell, and Killinger told him that he wanted to write a letter home.

The officer agreed, but told him that all he could say was that he was in St. Petersburg, was well, and was being well treated. Any return correspondence from Germany was to be addressed to the commanding officer at St. Petersburg. Obviously the Russians did not want the outside world to know exactly where he was. That was unsettling because it meant that the Russians did not consider Killinger and von Gorrissen to be regular prisoners of war. But obtaining permission to write a letter home had not been Killinger's true reason for wanting to speak with the officer. He needed a pen and paper to write messages to von Gorrissen, a critical part of the new communication plan he had devised.

Next he told the Russian officer that being in solitary confinement with nothing to do and nothing to read was driving him mad. Access to books was the second part of his plan. The officer agreed to provide books from the prison library and agreed to do the same for von Gorrissen. Because they did not read Russian they would receive books in French and Italian. Each man could order one book at a time. When he returned the book, he was allowed to take another one. Killinger's plan involved drawing books from the library according to a prearranged schedule so that he and von Gorrissen could shuttle messages back and forth. He used the pen and paper he had been given to write a letter home to explain the system to von Gorrissen, then slid the message into the book's spine and returned it to the library.

The next step was to tell von Gorrissen about the message and which author to ask for so that he could recover it. That night Killinger tapped a Morse code message that said, "Maupassant message inside." The coded message had to be short in order for him to send it within the brief time that the guard was away from his post. But brevity carried a price. If the library had more than one book by Maupassant, von Gorrissen might ask for the wrong one.

Several things had to happen for Killinger's new communications system to work. Von Gorrissen had to order the right book, find the message, and order the next designated book on the list. When he was done with that book he would put a message in the spine and return it to the library so that Killinger could order it and recover von Gorrissen's message. Killinger waited two days, ordered the next book, and found a message from von Gorrissen in the spine. The system worked! Eight days after losing their exercise privileges Killinger and von Gorrissen had reestablished regular contact with one another. It was slow, but it was the best system they had.

Confinement was taking its toll on both men. Von Gorrissen fell ill with a high fever and vomiting, and became so weak that he could no longer communicate with Killinger via the library book postal system. His last message told Killinger that he was ill, but did not tell him he was suffering from influenza and pneumonia. He was, in fact, very close to dying.

The sudden break in communications came at a time when Killinger was having his own health problems. The bayonet wounds in his left hand and chest, already infected, were getting worse because the Russians were providing no medical treatment and were withholding washing privileges in an attempt to make him talk. He had not had a bath or a shower since his capture, and the Russians' refusal to allow him to wash himself may have exacerbated both the infections and his scabies.

Desperate now, Killinger confronted the interrogation officer again, telling him that if he and von Gorrissen died as a result of not receiving medical treatment, they would be unable to give the Russians any of the information they wanted. There was certainly a grim logic in that, but it also depended on how important getting the information was to the Russian. He did not tell the Russian that he would talk in exchange for medical treatment; he simply said that if he died, he could not talk.

Maybe the Russian saw the logic in his argument, but it was more likely that he assumed Killinger was agreeing to talk in exchange for better treatment. Whatever the Russian thought, that day a doctor brought Killinger a bucket of clean water and a small bar of soap. The doctor smeared a paste on the left hand's wound and wrapped the hand in a clean bandage, but he ignored the chest wound, which remained untreated and uncovered.

The scabies was another matter. In fractured German the doctor told Killinger that his skin rash was scabies and gave him a laxative, perhaps thinking a laxative was better than nothing. The doctor returned twice to treat Killinger's infected hand and chest wound, and the wounds healed fairly quickly. But the laxative had no effect on the scabies.

The daily interrogations continued. Killinger was surprised and bewildered when his interrogator kept coming back to the *Friedrich Carl*. During one session the Russian told him that a Russian agent had recently seen the ship in Danzig. Aware that the cruiser had gone down after hitting a mine off Memel in 1914, and almost certain that the Russians knew that as well, Killinger simply told the Russian that he was not surprised to hear it. Killinger was just starting to understand the Russian's interrogation technique, and he realized that the interrogator was obtaining information even when the conversation appeared harmless. So he stopped talking altogether. The interrogator's demeanor changed from friendly to puzzled. He shook his head as though he could not understand why Killinger was being so stupid. He warned Killinger that continued silence could be dangerous.

The interrogator left the room and returned several minutes later with a more senior officer, who told Killinger that because he had killed innocent civilians, including children, when he bombed the Libau train station, he was to be hanged. The senior officer turned to leave, speaking sharply to the interrogator as he went through the door. The interrogator returned Killinger to his cell without saying another word to him.

He remained in his cell until evening, when two armed guards entered his cell and handcuffed his hands behind his back. The escort took him back to the interrogation room, where the senior officer was waiting. Without preamble the Russian gave him a last chance to make a statement.

When Killinger remained silent, the officer asked, "Do you have any wishes?" Killinger shook his head and was returned to his cell.

It was a difficult night. He truly believed that the Russians were going to hang him in the morning. He questioned the wisdom of remaining silent about information that in fact might have little, if any, military value. But that was just a passing thought. Killinger was a product of his time, upbringing, and naval training, which together reinforced a powerful sense of duty and personal honor.

No one came for him the following morning, and as the days dragged on he spent less and less time worrying about being executed. Four weeks passed without any word from or about von Gorrissen. The last information Killinger had received about his friend was that he was weak and had an unbroken high fever, and the silence worried Killinger deeply. He wondered if the Russians had simply let him die. In time he would learn that the Russians had moved von Gorrissen to a different prison.

At the end of Killinger's seventh week in the Peter and Paul Fortress, a German-speaking noncommissioned officer (NCO) entered his cell with his old uniform, now cleaned and pressed. While Killinger dressed, the NCO told him that he was being moved to a new place. Killinger hesitated for a moment. The last time he had spoken to the interrogator he had been told that he was to be executed. That might explain the fresh uniform and the move. When he was dressed, the NCO escorted him out of the cell, through the series of iron doors, and into bright sunlight. They exited the fortress and climbed into a waiting car, Killinger in the backseat between two soldiers, the NCO in the front passenger seat.

Nothing was said during the short drive, which ended in front of a two-story building. Killinger immediately noticed the two guards near the front door; both were well turned out and looked like regular army. The building had the appearance of a cheap hotel, the sort one found near railroad stations. The outer walls were soft yellow and white, and the green roof had several chimneys. In fact, the building *was* a hotel, or at least it had been before the war. Now it was a special camp for transient officer POWs.

Inside, the building was a substantial change from the gloomy prison. The few guards visible were friendly and relaxed; two were actually smoking on duty. The NCO led him down a well-lighted corridor to a ground-floor room and ushered him inside, saying that this was where he would be staying; then he left, locking the door behind him. The room was comfortably furnished with chairs, a table, and four beds. The window opened inward, but there was an iron grill covering the outside.

Killinger had figuratively gone from rags to riches overnight, and the sudden change in his circumstances should have raised an alarm. While he was still admiring his new quarters, two men entered the room through another door. Killinger was taken aback by their appearance. The men were dressed in nondescript clothes, and their hair and beards were long and unkempt. Speaking flawless German, one asked him, "Is it true that you are Herr Killinger?" Suspicion finally flared in Killinger's mind. He was in Russia, these two men looked like residents of a primeval forest, and they knew his name. He responded, "Are you Germans? And are you prisoners of war?"

Yes to both questions, the men told him. The man who had first spoken to Killinger was a chief petty officer who identified himself as Obermaschinist Ernst Lehmann. He had been the chief engineer on the Parseval semirigid airship PL-19 that had been shot down in January 1915 after bombing Libau. The other man, Obersteuermann Hermann Schack, was also a chief petty officer and had been the airship's navigator and helmsman. They told him that von Gorrissen had come to the house four days earlier and had told them about Killinger. In fact, they said, von Gorrissen was still there. The atmosphere immediately relaxed. The three men exchanged stories about how that had been captured and what they had experienced since. Of particular interest to all were the questions the Russians had asked and how everyone had answered those questions.

If what is written in Killinger's first book, *Die Abenteuer des Ostseefliegers*, is correct, the former hotel where they were housed was on the Neva River and very close to the tsar's palace. Killinger recalled:

> I was in paradise. I was again with men with whom I could speak, the room was comfortable, and we even had an iron stove for heat. The window overlooked the Neva River, and there was a well-tended garden behind the house in which we were allowed to walk for two hours each day.
>
> The guards were much friendlier than those at Peter and Paul Fortress had been, and we had access to an enormous supply of books. We also played chess, cards. The change in our situation was so great that I thought it must all be an illusion.

His joy was heightened when he learned that von Gorrissen was in the room adjacent to his, and that von Gorrissen's roommates were Oberleutnant zur See Ernst Meier, the PL-19's captain, and his first officer, Leutnant zur See Hermann Rotsold. Even better, he could talk to von Gorrissen through an open window whenever either of them took his daily two-hour walk in the garden. It was too good to be true. None of the prisoners who were housed in the building realized that the Russians were listening to and recording their conversations—even when they were outdoors in the garden.

They discussed an escape plan that involved breaking out the iron grill over the window, running through the garden to the Neva, and waiting there for the half-hourly patrol to pass. They would then swim across a "dead arm" of the river to a bridge and walk through the northern section of the city to open land. From there they would walk into Finland and on to the Gulf of Finland, where Killinger was sure they would find a vessel to take them to Sweden. He was also certain that the Finns were no friends of the Russians and would be helpful.

The first problem was their food supply—they would need enough to last several days; the second was their attire; and the third was where to get a file to cut through the bars. The first two problems were fairly easy to solve. Food for the escape could come from bread saved from their daily ration, which Killinger believed would last for a week if strictly rationed. They all agreed that their deep blue naval uniforms were not greatly different from a civilian's suit, especially if they removed the shoulder boards, sleeve stripes, and naval buttons.

Obtaining a file proved to be impossible, however, so they turned to making their own. They heated two table knives in a fireplace until they were red hot, then used one knife to hack "teeth" into the softened metal of the other. Then they reheated the knife and plunged it in cold water to temper it. The activity kept them occupied, but the plan did not work. The homemade file became instantly dull when they attacked the bars with it, and sharpening it proved to be a waste of time. In any event, the Russians knew all about the "file" and the plan. They had listened to it being made.

Audio technology was still primitive in World War I, but both sides used it widely to eavesdrop. The Germans had their own "listening hotel" in Karlsruhe where they listened to conversations among Allied officer POWs. Both intelligence-gathering centers operated on the same basis:

provide prisoners with comfortable accommodations, decent meals, and good company—and wire every room in the building. The Russians went one step further by extending their listening apparatus outside the barracks so they could hear what the prisoners had to say as they strolled the grounds.

The Russians apparently got the information they were after, because in the middle of the escape preparations they shipped Killinger, von Gorrissen, three NCOs from the PL-19, and four other officers to Siberia. The Russians told the Germans that they were going to the coal mines on Sakhalin Island and would spend the rest of their lives there.

A last-minute addition to their group was a naval infantryman who had been wounded in Flanders and sent to his home in Memel to recuperate. When the Russians attacked and briefly occupied the city in March 1915, he had volunteered to fight with the Landwehr defenders and the Russians captured him. Since then he had cooled his heels in the Peter and Paul Fortress, apparently forgotten. That was bad enough, but now he was lumped with a POW group that was being sent to the Sakhalin coal mines.

The Russians stuffed the ten prisoners into the back of a small van and drove to a train station. The city streets were brightly lighted in festive colors, and hordes of people were out. It appeared to Killinger that the Russians were celebrating another victory. The van pulled into the railyard and stopped next to a fourth-class coach where a Russian officer and eight soldiers were waiting for them. On 21 May 1915 they left St. Petersburg under heavy guard, headed east on the Trans-Siberian Railway.

As the POW experience goes, Erich Killinger had not been badly treated up to this point, though his stay in Peter and Paul Prison was hardly pleasant. The Russians had threatened him with shooting and hanging, and they had withheld medical treatment in an attempt to force him to talk. His wounds were painful but not life threatening, and the Russians had sent a doctor to treat them before the infection became really serious. Von Gorrissen had been very ill, but the Russians had already improved his circumstances before Killinger had his confrontation with the interrogator.

Later in life, Killinger had reason to reassess his POW experience. He concluded that withholding medical treatment in his case might not have been a violation of the two conventions that governed the treatment of prisoners of war—the Geneva Convention of 2 August 1864 and Hague II of 29 July 1899—but he came away convinced that withholding medical treatment to force a prisoner to talk was morally wrong. He was ambivalent about the threats the Russians made to hang him, which he believed had been generally ineffective and were utterly pointless when used on a prisoner who had a strong sense of duty. Though he disliked being in solitary confinement, he recognized it as a useful interrogation tool when combined with other softening-up techniques.

What most impressed him was the psychology behind suddenly improving a prisoner's living conditions, which had been so effective in his own case. He knew that he had told the chatty interrogator more than he should have, but he did not know that the Russians had learned much more from the bugged rooms he and his companions occupied.

TRANSPORTED EAST

21 May–8 October 1915

There were twenty-five German POWs in the railcar, including the seven-man crew from the PL-19: the captain, Oberleutnant zur See Ernst Meier; his executive officer, Leutnant zur See Hermann Rotsold; the ship's helmsman, Obersteuermann Hermann Schack; the chief engineer, Obermaschinist Ernst Lehmann; the second engineer, Maschinisten-Maat Wilhelm Gissov; and a Lutheran minister, Rev. Dr. Roetzell.[1]

Reverend Roetzell's presence on the PL-19 on 25 January 1915 was another hard-luck story. He was a civilian who had volunteered to be an interservice chaplain in Königsberg, and his congregation included the navy's airship station there. On the trip that ended in disaster for the PL-19 and its crew, he was just along for the ride, curious to know what it was like to fly in a gasbag and wanting to interact with the crew. Fortunately for him, the Russians assumed he was a sailor because he was wearing a cold-weather flight suit when he was captured with the others, and they treated him as a common POW. Had they known he was a civilian, they might have shot him as a franc-tireur.

The fourth-class rail carriage in which the POWs found themselves was typical of those common throughout European railways at the time. Just a step above a cattle car, the carriages were generally used for short trips by the lower classes, often to transport themselves, their produce, and their animals to local markets. The seats were bare wooden benches, and straw covered the floor. Each car had eight fairly large windows on each side and a platform at both ends protected by a domed overhang.

The guards told them that they were going to Vladivostok, a distance of more than four thousand miles. Killinger knew people who had made the trip from Vladivostok to St. Petersburg before the war by first-class railcar, and all had described a long and tiresome journey of about twelve days. Since they were obviously not going to be traveling first class, the Germans naively estimated that they would be under way for about twenty days. They had no idea yet of the vast distance they would cross and the unimaginable inefficiency of the Russian railway system.

Initially, Killinger found the trip interesting. The train passed through enormous forests, and he marveled at Russia's wealth in timber. But as days passed and they continued to slowly move eastward, the Germans began to realize that the journey was going to last much longer than twenty days. In fact, allowing for long stops at POW compounds along the way, the trip to Vladivostok would take more than six months.

Within a few days of getting under way the Germans developed a friendly relationship with their guards, who became extremely lax, apparently unconcerned that the prisoners might try to escape. They even allowed the POWs to stand outside on the end platforms and sit on the steps; and when the train stopped at a settlement each day for water, the guards allowed them to roam the town freely. As the prisoners got off the train, the guard commander gave each officer prisoner one ruble and fifty kopeks to buy food, the stipend conforming to existing conventions dealing with officer prisoners. But those same conventions said nothing about stipends for enlisted men, so the officers used part of their money to buy supplies for them as well. Much of the money went for items that would make their lives as prisoners easier: a large teapot to brew hot tea as well as pots and pans, bedding, and clothing.

The purchases underscore the fact that these men were not thinking about escape; they were thinking about making their enforced stay in Russia as comfortable as possible. That attitude was common among prisoners of war; in fact, fewer than 1 percent of World War I POWs ever attempted to escape. Most simply hunkered down and made the best of whatever came their way.[2] World War I produced approximately 8 million POWs, and 1 percent of that number would be 80,000. The actual number of World War I POWs who tried to escape is not known, but it was much lower than 80,000.

A major factor that inhibits thoughts about escaping—and it was definitely in play on the train trip east—is the apparent hopelessness of even trying. Very few prisoners will attempt escape if there seems to be no chance of getting away. The Germans knew nothing at all about the area they were traversing, except that it was a long way from Germany. They believed at this point that escape was not feasible, and they were probably right.

The daily excursions into the towns while the train took on water and coal continued as they progressed eastward. Some of the stops lasted several hours, during which the prisoners were completely unattended. On one occasion, when the train had stopped in a fairly large town, Killinger and three men from the PL-19—Meier, Rotsold, and Schack—came upon a large, well-built building that was obviously an officers' club. A man with several performing bears was outside, and the show had attracted a large crowd. The four Germans joined them and enjoyed the show so much that they lost track of time. After several hours they realized that the train might have left without them, and headed back to the station at the double—only to find that the train was still there and no one had even missed them.

Some of the officers' stipend went to buy Russian peasant blouses— loose shirts tightly cinched around the waist with a belt. That attire, combined with their long, unkempt hair and beards, allowed them to pass for locals. That no one paid any attention to them in the towns and that the guards had become quite lax naturally led to talk about escape.

Unexpectedly, Killinger argued against the idea. They still had no idea where they were. Were they in European or Asiatic Russia? They had no rations and lacked reliable maps or a compass. Without the latter they did not know which way to go or what lay in front of them—they would be fleeing into the unknown. And at that point Killinger believed that none of them spoke Russian. In short, he saw little or no possibility of success.

The chances of any escaped prisoner walking out of European Russia during World War I were poor, but it was not impossible to do. But the farther east they went, the more difficult successful escape became; and success meant reaching Germany. Killinger was not yet desperate enough to take the chance, but that time was coming.

At the end of three weeks the train passed through the Urals. The guard commander told the POWs that they would arrive in Omsk the following day and would be staying there for some time. The announcement was a pleasant surprise for Killinger and the PL-19 crew. They were going to a POW camp in Omsk instead of the coal mines on Sakhalin? The apparent change in destination sounded even better when the Russian guard described the conditions in Omsk as very good, adding that officers were billeted with citizens in the town or on farms near the town. They would be required to report to the camp commander every three days; otherwise they were free to do as they wished. They could even start small businesses.

Either the Russian's estimate of how far they were from Omsk was way off the mark or he overestimated the train's average speed. Perhaps he had never been this way before. In fact, they had traveled about 1,100 miles, and Omsk was still 600 miles away. The train arrived there eight days later, on 20 June 1915, and the prisoners realized almost immediately that the Russian who had promised good conditions was either poorly informed or an outright liar. The camp was anything but the paradise he had described.

The reality came as a shock, largely because Killinger and the others had been lulled by the relaxed treatment they had experienced during the past three weeks and by their inherent desire to hope for the best. Killinger later recalled their disappointment "when after an hours-long march through hot sand we arrived at a camp surrounded by high wooden palisades." The camp's occupants were mostly Austrians and Hungarians, with a sizable number of Turks, plus thirty Germans, including some who had recently arrived from St. Petersburg.

Most of the Austrians, Hungarians, and Germans had been captured in 1914, and they were eager to hear the latest news. There was not much good to tell, but the war news was not all bad, and it was current to 6 April 1915. Being the most recent captives among the new arrivals, Killinger and von Gorrissen did most of the talking.

They passed on the news that the Germans had won the First Battle of the Masurian Lakes in September 1914, but the Russians had quickly recovered and decisively stopped a renewed German attempt to cross the Niemen River, forcing the Germans to fall back to their entrenched lines at the Masurian Lakes. The Ninth Army had been formed on 19 September in Breslau in German Silesia, and von Hindenburg was given command of it, turning the Eighth Army over to General der Artillerie Richard von Schubert. The Germans had learned that Grand Duke Nikolay Nikolayevich Romanov of Russia, commander in chief of the Russian armies, was planning a massive offensive toward Kraków and into German Silesia, which required von Hindenburg to send forces to support Austria. General von Schubert was assigned to hold East Prussia while von Hindenburg took the Ninth Army to rescue the Austrians. Von Schubert was apparently not suited for command of the Eighth Army, and the more dynamic General der Infanterie Hermann von François relieved him on 9 October. Before the Ninth Army started its move south, General der Kavallerie August von Mackensen took command of the Ninth Army from von Hindenburg, who had been elevated to supreme commander of the east. On 2 November von Hindenburg was promoted to field marshal.

In January 1915 the German Ninth Army attacked the Russian Second Army under General Smirnov near the Polish village of Bolimów, on the Łódź-Warsaw Railway line. The Germans used chemical gas for the first time in World War I at Bolimów. What the newcomers were unable to tell the others was that the gas was xylyl bromide, a form of tear gas, and that seven pounds of the gas, together with a burster charge to scatter it, had been put into 18,000 6-inch shells. The attack failed because the gas did not vaporize in the cold winter air. Some of the gas was blown back toward the German lines, and some settled harmlessly to the ground. Many of the Russian soldiers were unaware that they had been attacked with gas and assumed that the barely audible explosions were the result of faulty ammunition.

The next flare-up had occurred in February and March 1915, starting with the Second Battle of the Masurian Lakes on 7–22 February 1915. The battle ended in another German victory. The Russian Tenth Army was destroyed, and the Germans took 110,000 prisoners. It was a tactical victory, not a strategic one; the Germans had fought to exhaustion.[3]

The news was encouraging for the camp residents, but even with the newcomers' emphasis on Germany's successes, the overall message was that the war was going to be a long one. And for the prisoners in Omsk, that meant it would be a long time before they saw their homes again.

When the St. Petersburg transport arrived in Omsk, some of the German POWs had been without a bath or a shower for nearly five months, and Killinger and von Gorrissen had gone without washing for more than ten weeks. They smelled like goats, and their hair and beards were dirty and tangled. The prisoners were dismayed to learn that there were no showers or baths in Omsk, either. According to Killinger, Omsk was one of the worst camps in Siberia. It was overcrowded, filthy, and almost entirely lacking in sanitation of any kind. There was one latrine for more than three hundred men and no medical care other than what the prisoners could provide themselves. Disease was rampant, especially cholera and typhus. Housing for the prisoners consisted of a one-story stone building with a single open bay that was virtually devoid of comfort. There were no chairs, tables, or mattresses. Double-deck wooden sleeping platforms extended the length of the building on both sides. The prisoners slept fully clothed on straw, and huddled together for warmth. The enlisted men detailed to the officers as orderlies had it particularly bad. They had to sleep either on the stone floor or outside on the stone steps.

Every morning the officers gathered outside the barracks, stripped to the waist, and examined their shirts for lice. It was a futile task because their clothing teemed with the tiny pests. One officer claimed to have killed 350 in one sitting. There was, however, some relief with respect to filthy clothing. The Russians allowed the Czech prisoners to live outside the compound in the Russian railroad camps. This practice was probably what the train guard commander was talking about when he described Omsk to Killinger and his companions as a paradise. The Czech prisoners came to the camp every morning to sell the Austrian prisoners cigarettes, food, and other items they lacked. One of the services that Czech entrepreneurs offered was a laundry service. Not everyone could afford it, and no one could afford it on a regular basis, but those who could occasionally take advantage of the service enjoyed at least temporary relief.

The biggest problem for the German prisoners in Omsk was that the Russians did not feed them. Omsk was a camp for Austrian and Hungarian prisoners; the Germans were transients en route to camps farther east, and the Russian camp commander apparently felt that he was not responsible for their care. It is also probable that he was selling the food intended for transient prisoners. Whatever the reason, the Germans had to depend almost entirely on the charity of their Austrian and Hungarian comrades. What food they could not get from the Austrians and Hungarians they had to scrounge or buy from the Czech prisoners, whom the Russians treated much better than the others.

The camp commander issued passes to the Czechs that allowed them to enter and exit the camp at will. Some of the Austrian and German prisoners had made counterfeit passes for themselves so that they could shop in the nearby railroad tent village. The availability of several camp-made stamps and seals made counterfeiting a pass relatively easy. An officer who regularly used a counterfeit pass told Killinger that the Russian guards were illiterate, and if the stamps and seals on the counterfeit looked good enough they would allow the bearer free access in and out of the camp.[4]

The only problem was that the user of a counterfeit pass had to wear a Czech uniform because even an illiterate guard could recognize the difference between Czech uniforms and those the Germans and Austrians wore. The solution was to rent a Czech prisoner's uniform for a couple of hours. The Czech who rented his uniform had to remain in the camp until the renter returned it. Since the camp commander held only two roll calls a day, one in the morning and one at dusk, the switch went undetected.

In addition to the pleasure of simply being outside the palisades, Killinger was able to buy potatoes and an occasional egg in the tent village. But the greatest reward was being able to strip and bathe in the river. Other than in and around the train station, there were few Russian soldiers in the tent village, and none went down to the river. The tent village residents and the few soldiers who were in the village were so accustomed to seeing the Czech prisoners moving about freely that no one bothered with him.

Even with the advantage of an occasional foray out of the camp, the POW compound at Omsk was a hellhole. Fortunately for Killinger and his fellow travelers from St. Petersburg, after twenty days they were told to gather their things and move out. They were to be part of a large transport making the next step toward POW camps located deep in Siberia.

The prisoners—30 Germans and 120 Turks—were loaded into cattle cars that departed Omsk on 11 July 1915 for a 14-day trip. The conditions on the train were a preview of the harsher conditions they would face in Siberia. This time there was no getting off the train during the fuel and water stops. The train made one stop each day in the middle of nowhere. The Russian guards went down the line of cars, unlocking and sliding the doors open, allowing the prisoners to climb down from the car for a brief period to exercise, relieve themselves, and clean out their filthy cars. At each stop the prisoners were under heavy guard.

One day on this trip Killinger witnessed an example of either Russian pragmatism and field expediency or institutionalized inefficiency and waste. Thousands of German POWs witnessed the same thing during and after World War II while they were prisoners in the Soviet Union. The train stopped, and the guards ordered all the prisoners out of their cars. While the prisoners were being assembled, the train crew disconnected the rear coupling on a disabled car in the middle of the train. The engineer backed the train a short distance, stopped, and allowed the cars that had been uncoupled to roll freely down the track. The train crew disconnected the front coupling on the disabled car, and the engineer moved the train forward, leaving the car standing alone on the track, smoke curling from a hot wheel bearing.

The guards directed the prisoners to gather on one side of the car and push against it in order to tip it off the track. There were so many prisoners that they got in each other's way, though, and the number of men who could actually push on the car lacked the collective strength to do the job. The solution lay in using two very long, heavy posts as levers while the prisoners pushed against the side of the car. Even then, it took nearly an hour before the car toppled off the tracks and lay on its side on the embankment.

Killinger was "pleasantly surprised" when the train arrived in Udinsk, Siberia, on 25 July 1915. Udinsk was a vast improvement over Omsk. The "prison camp" was simply a collection of individual houses that sat in an unenclosed forest clearing; there were no walls, fences, or barbed wire. Not only was the camp completely open, there were no guards to be seen. They were there, of course, but none of them manned guard posts, and they rarely made an appearance in the camp. If ever there was a POW camp designed to simply walk away from, this was it.

The lack of fences and guards should have given the new arrivals a clue that this camp was, in a practical sense, escape-proof. No one walked away from it because the camp was in such a remote part of the world that reaching Germany or Austria was impossible, even if the escapee knew which way to go. And the decent conditions in the camp made the risks and hardships of hiking through hostile country to Austria or Germany an unappealing choice.

Killinger described the officers' quarters, in which four officers were assigned to a room, as "friendly, well-lighted rooms that we decorated to suit our tastes. The Austrians were very helpful and provided us with whatever we needed to set up housekeeping." Each room was provided with two oversized cots, mattresses, and blankets. The cots were oversized because the prisoners were expected to pair up for sleeping, a condition quite acceptable to males living under road conditions in the early twentieth century. Nor was food a problem at Udinsk. The officers' mess served a limited menu, mostly soup and black bread, but occasionally there was meat; and peasants living in the area were allowed to trade freely with the prisoners.

The bulk of the camp's population consisted of 2,500 Austrian enlisted men and 250 Austrian officers. When the Germans from Omsk arrived there were only twenty-two German POWs in the camp—twenty enlisted soldiers and two officers, both fliers. There were also several Gypsies who were not prisoners but had attached themselves to the camp much like camp followers. Among their other industries, the Gypsies had organized an orchestra, and there were Gypsy violinists for every occasion. The Austrians, who had been in the camp since shortly after the war started, had created an active woodworking industry that produced a host of wood products from furniture to violins.

The German officers were paid eighteen rubles a month but were expected to use the money to buy food and other necessities at the camp canteen, which the Russians operated. Prices were high and the eighteen rubles did not go very far, but at least the men were being paid regularly, something that had not been the case so far. In fact, thanks to the Austrians, the German officers did better than just eighteen rubles a month. The Austrian officers each received fifty rubles a month, and the three Austrian generals in the camp set up a special account for the Germans into which each Austrian officer paid a fixed monthly amount. At the start of each month, the money in that account was divided among the German officers, raising their monthly income to twenty-eight rubles a month.

The Russian in command of the camp was an officer candidate who had worked in Shanghai before the war and spoke excellent German. He was well over the usual age for a cadet, and Killinger suspected that he had been given the rank and the assignment solely on the basis of his ability to speak German. In any event, he was a fortunate choice for the prisoners because he was a fair and generous man. He went so far as to provide the Austrians with a coffee house that offered coffee, tea, cakes, and even ice cream. The camp commander was readily available to discuss almost any issue. Through conversations with him, Killinger formed a general idea of what lay between Udinsk and China, and also of the attitudes of the Chinese toward foreigners in general and Germans in particular. Killinger concluded that the earlier train guard commander had confused Omsk with Udinsk.

Improved living conditions were not the only advantage to being in Udinsk. Many Austrian officers had managed to conceal their maps when they surrendered to the Russians and had smuggled them into the camp. The maps allowed Killinger to put Udinsk in geographical perspective. A line drawn from Udinsk due south ran right through the middle of Mongolia and China. Due north lay a vast, frozen wasteland, and due east was another frozen wasteland that reached to the Pacific Ocean. Europe and Germany were due west but much too far away to reach on foot. Like those who had arrived there ahead of him, Killinger concluded that Udinsk was not a likely place to mount an escape attempt, which is why the Russians did not see a need to guard the camp.

The guard detachment in the camp was constantly changing as men were called to the front and replaced by new guards who quickly became part of the relaxed camp life. Every guard who left for the front obtained a note called a *bumaga* from a German or Austrian officer attesting to the guard's friendliness toward German and Austrian POWs and the good treatment he had given them. The guards hoped that the notes would make life easier if they became POWs, and Killinger believed that many of them planned to cross over to the German lines and surrender voluntarily. The Germans did not give away the *bumaga*; they exchanged the individual recommendations for a variety of goods, including up-to-date maps.

It was on the basis of information he obtained from the Russian maps that Killinger decided to wait until he was shipped to a camp farther east and closer to the coast before attempting to escape. The land closer to the coast was more populated, which meant greater access to food and shelter as he moved south; and most Chinese cities had a German consulate, which would be a source of much-needed help.

The prisoners were naturally interested in what was happening at the front, and an active intelligence operation sprang up in Udinsk to keep them informed. Austrian officers who spoke and read Russian obtained news from Russian newspapers that the guards supplied in trade for *bumaga*. They dispensed the intelligence to the camp through a daily camp newspaper and an oversized situation map that was "meticulously" kept up-to-date with colored pushpins. Killinger was in charge of moving the pins. He also published the daily camp newspaper, which sold for two kopeks a copy. The printing was done in his room using glue, gelatin, and two cookie sheets. The hectograph method he used was a transfer process using special inks and a gelatin pad. Where Killinger obtained the necessary supplies to print the paper his books do not say. But since a Russian,

Mikhail Alisov, invented the hectograph in 1869 and the invention was widely used, it is probable that the materials were available either in the camp or through barter with the locals.

The news was not always accurate or up-to-date, but the intelligence gathering was efficient enough that the camp knew in August 1915 that a German and Austro-Hungarian offensive had opened between Gorlice and Tarnów on 2 May 1915. How effective the offensive was remained unknown for several months, but on 30 August 1915 they received a clue when a stricter camp commander replaced the lenient one.

The new camp commander immediately instituted a policy of frequent and unannounced searches of the officers' quarters. Anticipating that the situation map and the newspaper printing supplies would be prime targets for the inspectors, Killinger and others hid them. They also practiced their own surprise inspections to train the lookouts and others involved what to do. The two cookie sheets were simply hung on a peg on the kitchen wall, and the glue and gelatin were stored with the food supplies in containers marked as something else. The ready-to-distribute newspapers and the "press" were hidden inside the iron woodstove that heated the room. Since it was summer, the stove was unused and the flue was cold. Though it was now more difficult, the intelligence service continued to gather information and Killinger continued to print it.

The new commander had little effect on the monotony of life in the camp. Clouds of mosquitoes and stifling heat continued to make life there uncomfortable throughout the summer. The two bright points were that typhus and cholera were never a problem in Udinsk, and the new camp commander did not restrict the daily barter with the peasant farmers who brought goods to the camp.

September brought the first snow, heralding the bitter cold to come. The arrival of winter coincided with news that the Entente's May offensive had driven the Russians back to a line that ran from Riga on the Baltic to Czernowitz on the Romanian border. The Russian reverses also brought command decisions that made life miserable for the Germans in Udinsk, including cutting the German officers' pay. With winter came disease, the worst being scurvy, which killed many prisoners who were not prepared for the winter. The German POWs complained to the governor in Irkutsk, who made a personal visit to the camp. The Germans deluged him with complaints about the camp commander's fraud and vindictiveness.

In reaction to the military setbacks and the Germans' complaints, the Russians shipped all the German officers in Udinsk to a reprisal camp at Spassk, about one hundred miles north of Vladivostok. The trip was to be made by train along the Trans-Siberian Railway, a route that would take Killinger into Manchuria.

ESCAPE

8–28 October 1915

A glance at a map told the forty German officers they were in for a long train ride. It was 8 October 1915 when the Russians told them to gather their belongings and move out. Anticipating a long, cold trip, they took everything they could carry. The men who assembled outside the barracks for the march to the train were a ragtag bunch. Every man had a mattress tied on his back and carried a large pot filled with cooking utensils and food, and at least one piece of furniture, either a small table or a stool. They looked more like refugees than German officers.[1]

The train was made up entirely of cattle cars, most of which were already packed with Russian peasants who were being "relocated" to Siberia. The peasants were ostensibly going east with promises of new land, but the conditions of their travel made it clear to the Germans that these people were simply being deported. The peasants had already been under way for two months, and their condition was pitiful. They were dressed in rags, starving, and suffering terribly from the bitter cold.

Compared to the peasants, the Germans were going first class. They were assigned to two boxcars at the end of the train, both equipped with an iron stove and firewood. With only twenty men in a car there was ample room to set up housekeeping and settle in for the long haul. The iron stove, set in the middle of the floor, was a godsend that literally kept the Germans from freezing. The nighttime temperature was already –20° Celsius.

The daily routine included a stop each day to take on fuel and water, during which the passengers were allowed out of their cars. The stops occasionally provided the Germans with opportunities to buy food and other supplies, but the deported Russians were denied that opportunity because they had no money and nothing to trade. Killinger was distressed at what he saw: "The sight of those ragged, emaciated, shivering people was terrible. The Russians had packed them into the cattle cars without regard to age or physical condition. Many died during the trip from hunger and cold, and at every stop the dead were laid alongside the track. They came to us at every opportunity and knelt down, tugging at our clothing, begging for something to eat. The train guards drove peasants along with heavy blows of their *nagaika* whips. So this is how the Russian government cares for its people."

The peasants' condition gave the Germans an inkling of what was in store for them. Killinger felt the first pangs of desperation as he realized that his only hope for survival was escape, and he resolved to get away no matter what the obstacles might be. Others shared his desperation and resolve.

Despite the stress associated with the trip, the 124-mile stretch from Udinsk to Lake Baikal was pleasant enough for the Germans. They had sufficient food and enough fuel to keep their cars warm. The guards did not lock the doors, and the Germans sometimes slid them open during the day and viewed the country through which they were passing.

After one stop the men realized that one of their company was missing. The man had gone into the station and was still there when the train pulled out. He boarded an express train that stopped at the station later in the day and rode on the platform of the last car for two days, passing the POW train along the way. The truant prisoner simply got off at the express train's next stop and waited for the POW train to catch up. The Russians had not missed him. The experience fueled the Germans' interest in escaping and raised their expectations for success.

It took three days to get around the south end of the Baikalsee, and Killinger found the scenery awe inspiring: "In terms of the landscape, this was the most beautiful trip I had ever taken. The lake is ringed with high, steep granite mountains whose wild, snow-capped summits remind one of the Swiss Alps. In one moment the train is traveling immediately along the lake's shore and then suddenly is climbing up the granite mountain and clinging to a sheer stone face with the deep blue lake far below." As the train left Lake Baikal behind, the landscape changed to steppes and the signs at the stations were increasingly in Mongolian and Chinese. They even saw camel caravans in the distance. As the train neared the Chinese border, the Germans formed groups to discuss and plan escapes. Someone told the others that the Trans-Siberian Railway was not yet completed through Russian territory, and they must therefore pass through neutral Manchuria. It seemed the ideal place to jump from the train because their chances of successfully evading recapture would be much improved if they landed in neutral territory. The prospect raised morale considerably and added urgency to their escape preparations.

It was true that Manchuria was a neutral country, but the part of China in which they would have to make their escape was crawling with Russian and Japanese troops. In 1896 China granted Russia a concession to build a single-track "Manchurian shortcut" running from the Siberian city of Chita to the Russian port of Vladivostok. The route drastically reduced the travel distance that would have been required along the Trans-Siberian Railway's originally proposed main northern route to Vladivostok. The unfinished northern route lay completely inside Russia and was not completed until many years after the shortcut came into use.[2]

The Chita-Vladivostok shortcut was part of the larger Chinese Eastern Railway–building program through northern Manchuria. When completed in 1902 the southern branch of the Chinese Eastern Railway consisted of three branches: the western branch, Manzhouli to Harbin; the eastern branch, Harbin to Suifenhe; and the southern branch, Harbin to Peking. The entire concession was known as the Chinese Eastern Railway Zone, but it was the Russians who administered it from Harbin.

At the same time they built the shortcut the Russians also built a 550-mile-long line running south from Changchun down the Liaodong Peninsula to Lushun, where they were building Port Arthur, a strategic naval base and marine coaling station for Russia's Far East Fleet. To protect the concession and to ensure there would be no Chinese interference with its operation, Russian troops occupied northern Manchuria. The 1904 Russo-Japanese War was fought largely over who would control this region and Port Arthur. After losing that war, Russia lost both the Liaodong Peninsula and much of the South Manchurian Railway's southern branch to Japan. The rail line from Changchun to Lushun was transferred to Japanese control and became the South Manchurian Railway. Despite losing control of a large part of their concession area, the Russians continued to control the Chita-Vladivostok shortcut and maintained a strong troop presence in the area throughout World War I.

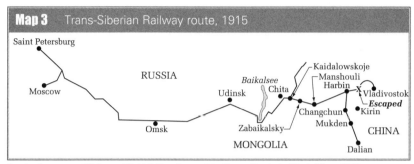

Based on Department of Railways, *Official Guide to Eastern Asia: Chosen, Manchuria, Siberia* (Tokyo, 1900).

The Japanese-controlled South Manchurian Zone was a 200-foot-wide strip of land on both sides of the South Manchurian Railway tracks extending along the 435-mile main trunk route from Dalian to Chang-chun, the 160-mile Mukden-Antung route, and 4 other spur routes, for a total length of 685 miles and a total land area of 150 square miles. These rail lines connected twenty-five cities and towns that featured warehouses, repair shops, coal mines, and electrical facilities to operate the railway.

Like Russia, Japan stationed troops to provide security for the trains and tracks throughout the South Manchurian Zone, including in the cities and towns. The troops were not really railroad guards, as they were called, but rather regular Japanese soldiers who frequently conducted military maneuvers outside the railway areas. In addition, Japan also maintained consular police attached to the Japanese consulates and branch consulates in major cities throughout the occupied area.

After several monotonous days of traveling through the vast, empty land, the train stopped at a small station and the Germans got off to look around. The guards ignored them, probably content that the prisoners had nowhere to go in this wasteland. While the others were scrounging supplies, Killinger entered the station. The building was deserted, and as he looked around he spotted a Trans-Siberian Railway map tacked to the wall. Without hesitating he strode across the room, pulled the map off the wall, and shoved it inside his coat.

As soon as he was back inside the boxcar he examined his treasure closely. The map was in Russian, dated 1903, and was not up-to-date, but it clearly defined the railroad route and showed the border between Russia and China. Most important, the map showed a fork in the line a few miles east of Chita. One track, the Trans-Siberian Railway, curved north along the Amur River; the other track, which the Chinese Eastern Railway Company shared, curved southeast into Manchuria and continued eastward across northern China for more than seven hundred miles, passing through Harbin before reentering Russia at Suifenhe. From there the line went on to Vladivostok.[3]

If the train took the northern track, it would remain in Russia and would pass close to two large POW camps at Srjetensk and Blagowjeschtschensk, making escape difficult, if not impossible. Given that the northbound line was actually a dead end, since it was still unfinished and would not take them to Vladivostok, it seemed unlikely that the train would follow it. On the other hand, the Russians had been dropping off the prisoners in prison camps along the way and might intend to drop the remaining Germans off at the two large camps on the northbound line. It seemed probable to Killinger that the Russians would put them off the train at either Srjetensk or Blagowjeschtschensk. Having no way of knowing which track the train would take, Killinger decided to make his decision as the train approached the fork.

During the time the train was rolling toward the fork, Killinger developed an escape plan. At this point he was working alone and apparently did not discuss his plan with von Gorrissen. He had watched the fast express trains that daily roared past while the POW train stood on a siding. He looked closely at each train as it went by, focusing on the trucks—the wheel and brake assembly that carried the railcar along the tracks—and came to the conclusion that he could easily wedge himself between the axle and the braking equipment.

His map showed a Chinese Eastern Railway Company track running south from Harbin to Mukden. He believed that if he escaped at Harbin, he could find a southbound passenger train, conceal himself under a car, and ride the axle for the 315-mile trip to Mukden. Finding a passenger train was central to his plan because he optimistically assumed that a fast passenger train would cover the distance in forty-eight hours, and he was convinced that he could hold on to the axle for two days without falling off.

During this time he observed six men, including von Gorrissen, spending a great deal of time with their heads together, studying and discussing a piece of paper. He correctly assumed that they were also planning an escape and approached them, saying, "Aha, you are also planning to escape." They showed Killinger the small map of Asia they had been examining. It lacked detail but showed the rivers and mountains with which they would have to deal. He showed them his purloined railroad route map, said that he was also going to escape, and joined the group.

He learned that the six favored jumping from the train west of Harbin and walking south to Mukden. When Killinger told them about his plan to ride on the axle beneath a railcar, they dismissed the idea as *"völlig unmöglich,"* utterly unworkable. Someone pointed out that no one could ride the axle in those frigid conditions without succumbing to the cold and losing his grip. Killinger saw the light and agreed that walking south was a better idea.

Now that they had Killinger's railroad map, the seven Germans were reasonably well equipped to plot their route. They did not have a compass, but all agreed that they had only to head south, a direction easily determined by watching the sun. Or so they thought. All agreed that if the train turned north at the fork, they would jump right then. The early jump would add several hundred miles to their walk, but there would be no other opportunity.

If, however, the train took the southern fork, they estimated that the 315-plus-mile trek south to Mukden would take 6 to 8 weeks. It was a surprisingly accurate estimate; most escapees greatly overestimate the speed at which they will travel. That they were all wearing German uniforms was not deemed a problem because they believed that the area they would pass through was sparsely populated and none of the inhabitants whom they might encounter would recognize their uniforms. It was also the case that their disreputable appearance after six months of captivity was anything but soldierly.

As the train rumbled slowly eastward, they begged and traded for food, better boots, a rucksack, and Russian money whenever the train stopped and they were able to mingle with the other German prisoners. But the thirty-three other prisoners were a small resource pool from which to draw supplies. Nevertheless, the seven scraped together forty rubles, a kitchen knife, and what they believed was enough bread, sugar, tea, and sausages to last eight days. They were being overly optimistic about their food supply, and getting enough to eat would be one of their toughest challenges.

They thought their chances of successful escape from the train were excellent. They were in the fourth car of a five-boxcar train, and the other twenty Germans were in the last car. The two cars ahead of them were jammed with Russian deportees, and the guards were all in the lead car, immediately behind the locomotive, where it was comfortable. The sliding doors on the cars carrying the Germans were not locked, and the prisoners could open them at will. The train traveled no more than forty miles per hour and often as slowly as fifteen miles per hour. Their jump from the train would be unobserved, and they would be jumping into fairly deep snow.

They continued gathering supplies but spent most of their time discussing the obstacles they would face once they were off the train. The second phase of their escape might last several weeks, depending on circumstances over which they had no control and could only guess at. The biggest unknown was the attitude of the people they would encounter. Would they be hostile, ambivalent, or cooperative? The safest course would be to remain largely unobserved, but they needed food and shelter, which were most likely to be found near people. They believed that remaining unobserved was not as critical as it would have been if they were escaping through Europe, but it was a concern. They planned to be on the march for up to eight weeks, and there was little food to be taken from the land, and temperatures would be well below freezing.

The obvious problems associated with walking several hundred miles through a hostile winter landscape without adequate provisions and clothing deterred three of the prisoners. One of the men who dropped out was von Gorrissen, whose health was so poor that he had little chance of surviving the march. That left Killinger; Oberleutnant Eberhard Brunn, a Grenadier Guards officer; Leutnant (Second Lieutenant) Kurt Cleinow, an army aerial observer; and Obermaschinist Ernst Lehmann from the airship PL-19.

Oberleutnant Brunn had been captured in September 1914 after crossing through no-man's-land under a flag of truce to arrange a temporary cease-fire so that both sides could recover their wounded and dead lying between the front lines. Instead of agreeing to the cease-fire, the Russians made Brunn a prisoner. He had been in Omsk when Killinger's group arrived there and was reasonably fit considering that he had been a prisoner for twelve months. He was at least as healthy as Killinger and Cleinow.

Leutnant Cleinow and his pilot, Oberleutnant Karl Lau, had been shot down on 3 October 1914 and had joined the train in Udinsk. Cleinow, the youngest member of the group, was also fairly healthy despite having been a POW for a year, and he possessed an invaluable tool—he spoke Russian.[4] At thirty-five Ernst Lehmann was the oldest member of the group, the others all being in their twenties. He had been a prisoner since January 1915, but despite his age he was in better physical condition than the others. He had been a laborer before joining the army, which might have prepared him physically for the ordeal of being a POW.

By 21 October 1915 the escape group was as well prepared as possible; they had some provisions, reasonably useful maps, a Russian-speaking member, and two men who knew how to navigate—Killinger and Cleinow. All that remained was to choose the right time to go, and that time would come shortly after the train passed through Kaidalowskoje, where the track forked.

As the train passed through Kaidalowskoje, Killinger peered out the window anxiously. He knew that if the train crossed the Ingoda River shortly after passing through Kaidalowskoje, it had taken the southern branch into Mongolia and was headed toward Vladivostok via Harbin. An hour or more after leaving Kaidalowskoje behind, the train rumbled onto a bridge. The situation started looking very good. Things looked even better when the train passed through the last Russian town, Zabaikalsky, before crossing the border into Mongolia.

More than four hundred miles remained between them and Harbin, and they discussed jumping somewhere along this stretch. But jumping from a train moving forty to forty-five miles an hour would risk serious injury. They entertained the idea of staying with the train until it stopped in Harbin and disappearing into the station crowd. If the Russians behaved as they had since the train left Udinsk, the absent prisoners would not be missed when the train pulled out. But the situation changed abruptly when the train stopped in the last Mongolian station, Manzhouli.

There the Russians ordered them out of their boxcars to meet a new guard commander and new guards. The new guards marched them to another platform where a train stood waiting and put them on a fourth-class car in the middle of the train. Before they boarded, a squad of Russian soldiers showed up and added two German officers to the group. Both men had been badly beaten and were bleeding from head wounds, the price for being recaptured after trying to escape.

The newcomers told a discouraging tale. A German-speaking Russian railroad employee had advised them to jump from their train while it was standing in the Harbin station, assuring them that they could easily disappear into the crowd and buy Mongolian horses that they could ride south. The two Germans believed the man but were immediately captured and severely beaten when they sprang off the train onto the station platform. The Russians had taken the two men west to Manzhouli and waited for the next eastbound train that had prisoners on board. The Russians were being coldly practical. The stretch between the fork and Harbin had already been the scene of several escape attempts and a few successful escapes—at least successful in the sense that the jumpers got away from the train without being killed or immediately recaptured. On the basis of their experience, the Russians had beefed up the security along that stretch of track and had adopted a policy of putting badly beaten escapees on the next eastbound train to serve as a warning to anyone who was thinking about jumping from the train.

The Russians also replaced the old guards with new ones who were much more vigilant. Before ordering the Germans into the fourth-class car, the guard commander drew his sword and threatened to behead any prisoner who attempted to escape. Once on the train the Germans discovered that the windows were locked with a type of throw-bolt, and the new Russian guard commander had placed five armed guards at each end of the car. They were told that no one would be allowed off the train when it stopped for fuel and water.

The only bright spot in the picture was that the train was definitely in Mongolia, which was nominally Chinese and neutral. The truth was, however, that the Russians and the Japanese controlled the railroads and the Chinese had little say about it. Despite the setback, the four men remained determined to make the break; the only matters to settle were when to go and how to get out. Now that the plan to escape into the crowd at Harbin station was no longer viable, they would have to jump.

At the increased speed the train was traveling, they estimated that the 437-mile leg from Manzhouli to Harbin would take four days. They chose to jump the night before the train arrived in Harbin, so they had to be ready to go in three days. Unknown to them, their train was traveling almost twice as fast as the train they had ridden from Udinsk, and they seriously underestimated the time it would take to reach Harbin.

As for how they would get out of the car, there were two options. One was to storm the rear door, overpower the guards, and jump. The other option was to simultaneously open four windows and jump. If they went out the door, the order in which they planned to leave the train was Killinger, Lehmann, Brunn, and Cleinow. Lehmann, who was the strongest, would be responsible for the rucksack with all their supplies.

Since the window exit was the more practical, they quietly prepared four windows for the escape. They successfully picked the window locks and greased the bolts so they would slide out silently. They also greased the window guides so the windows would easily and quickly slide upward. Every night one member of the group was always awake, watching the guards to determine the order in which they were rotated through the various guard positions.

On the second day they left Mongolia and entered Manchuria. The terrain along the track became marshy and swampy, which they judged was effectively impassable. Disappointed, they elected to postpone their escape until after the train had passed through Harbin. But the following afternoon, twenty-four hours earlier than they had anticipated, the train stopped in Harbin and remained in the station until 8 p.m. It was pitch black and snowing when the train pulled out so they had no opportunity to see the sort of terrain into which they would be jumping. For all they knew, it could be the same sort of swampy ground that had deterred them the previous day. Nevertheless, if they were going to go, they had to do it that night.

They decided to use only one window for their escape and firmed up the order in which they would go through it. Killinger would be first, followed by Lehmann, who would throw the rucksack containing all their supplies through the window and then jump, followed by Brunn and Cleinow. Each man would lie facedown after hitting the ground and remain so until the train had passed. As soon as the train rolled past, the last three out would run back along the tracks while Killinger would retrieve the rucksack and run toward them. It was agreed that anyone injured during the jump would be left behind.

That night the guard was increased, which turned out to be an unexpected blessing. Ten soldiers were jammed into the front of the car, blocking the exit and the platform; eight more guards choked the rear of the car. Shortly before 10 p.m. on 28 October 1915, while the train was moving at a very slow fifteen miles per hour, the other prisoners started a distraction by brawling at both ends of the car. The Russian guards were slow to react, being more interested in watching the fight than in restoring order. While their comrades exchanged blows and grappled in the aisle, Killinger stood up, opened the window, got both knees on the sill while clutching the window frame with his right hand, and pushed off, headfirst. As he dropped, the platform step on the next car clipped him on the right thigh, knocking him away from the train and causing him to land face-up in the snow. He quickly rolled facedown and buried his face in the snow until the train passed.

The rucksack, Lehmann, Brunn, and Cleinow came out of the window in rapid succession and fell into the snow. As they were coming out, Killinger was wondering if he had been injured and assuming that he must have been. Things were happening very fast now. The train was slowing to a stop a hundred yards down the track as Killinger sprang up and started running in the direction of the train, realizing that he was miraculously uninjured. He found the rucksack just as his three companions reached him. Cleinow was shouting, "Run, run!"

Meanwhile, the platform guard, seeing the bodies coming headfirst out the window and tumbling down the embankment, had pulled the emergency stop and fired after them. Now Russian soldiers were standing along the track and firing in the general direction of the escapees. The four men were just joining up when the heavy firing started, and Cleinow's shouted warning sent them away from the tracks, spreading out and running for their lives.

They had the advantage of a moonless night, and the train guards, who could not abandon the remaining prisoners, made no attempt at pursuit. After firing dozens of rounds into the dark, the Russians climbed back on board and the train resumed its journey. The success of the escape and immediate flight was a tonic to the four men. After a hurried check for injuries that revealed only "trivial abrasions," they immediately started their trek south.

They had successfully accomplished the least difficult phase of the escape; now they faced the second and much more difficult phase—evasion. Ahead of them lay nearly four hundred miles of hostile terrain, subzero weather, bandits, and Japanese troops. As though the next phase was not going to be difficult enough, in an act of incredible stupidity they discarded their gloves, scarves, and blankets to save weight.

EVASION

28 October–12 December 1915

With no immediate pursuit, the four escapees made good time until they came to a swamp. Unable to find a way around it in the dark, they spent the night huddled together and shivering in a stand of three-foot-high willows.[1] No one was able to sleep, and daylight brought no relief from the freezing cold. The only way to generate any warmth would be to start walking, but they chose to remain where they were, believing that they were still too close to the railroad to move safely during the day.

As the morning dragged on, it became obvious that remaining among the willows until dark would be fatal. Unless they began moving they would die of exposure in the subzero cold. A new storm that rolled in about noon bringing heavy snowfall and falling temperatures forced a decision. They pushed on, counting on the storm to hide them. During the evasion phase of their escape they had to avoid being seen, which would probably lead to recapture by the Russians, the Japanese, or the Chinese.

If the Russians captured them they would be sent back to Siberia. If the Japanese captured them they would either turn them over to the Russians or send them to a German POW camp in Japan. Neither prospect was attractive. If the Chinese captured them they might turn them over to either the Russians or the Japanese, or they might intern them in China for the duration of the war. Being interned in China might be better than being turned over to the Russians or Japanese, but the result—long-term confinement—would be the same. And the conditions would probably be no better than under the Russians or the Japanese.

There was also a threat of which they were unaware. The Russians paid a reward of twenty-five to fifty rubles to anyone who turned over an escaped POW. The threat of being turned in for the bounty in China was probably less than in Russia, but there was enough of a Russian presence in China to make the threat real.[2]

Avoiding recapture was crucial, but they also had to contend with being poorly clothed in subfreezing temperatures, which gave finding adequate shelter a higher priority than avoiding civilian contact. It was the cold rather than the need to avoid recapture that forced them to make their next decision.

It was growing dark when they came to a small peasant village that they approached cautiously. The villagers reacted with surprise, fear, and suspicion when they saw the four disreputable-looking Germans—perhaps the first Europeans they had ever seen. Using gestures to reassure the villagers of their peaceful intentions, the Germans managed to turn fear and suspicion into passive acceptance and curiosity. Again using gestures the Germans were finally able to convey their need for food and shelter.

One of the villagers led the Germans into his hut, where there was a smoldering fire, and offered them something to eat. Three of the escapees sat around the fire and ate while the fourth stood by the door watching for any sign that the peasants might try to harm them or turn them in to the authorities. To win the villagers' goodwill they offered them uniform buttons as gifts. Apparently it worked; the villagers ignored them thereafter and made no threatening moves.

The Germans remained in the hut until around midnight, when they again got under way, prompted by two considerations: every hour they marched brought them closer to their goal, and they were still uneasy about what the villagers might do. The fact that they had eaten and were warm made the decision to leave much easier.

They were still very cautious. Their experience during this first contact with locals was no assurance that they would receive the same reception in every village—and they found many more villages than they had anticipated. They had expected the region to be largely unpopulated, but found instead that there were villages at short intervals all along their way. For the next few days they continued to avoid the villages in favor of walking at night and hiding during the day. Their favored hiding places were cemeteries, which usually were in a stand of trees surrounded by large open spaces. Brunn had read that Chinese avoided cemeteries for fear of encountering ghosts. Whether or not that was true, they were never disturbed while hiding in a cemetery and continued using them whenever possible.

Soon, however, cold and hunger forced them to make contact again with the local peasants. The contacts became more frequent as the Germans became increasingly convinced that no harm would come to them. At first they approached only small villages and made contact with the people who lived in the outlying huts. As they became more confident they began to enter the larger villages, where there was more food and somewhat better accommodations. Near the end of the second week they were walking mostly during the day and taking shelter in a village at night. They found that the villagers would always provide shelter, but they did not always provide food—or enough of it.

The occasional relief they got from dealing with the locals did not reduce the hardships they faced as they pushed south. The temperature remained below freezing, they were inadequately clothed, and even with the food the villagers gave them they were starving. The brutal cold had frozen their meager provisions solid, and they had no way to thaw them. Though they had a few matches, they rarely found enough kindling to build a fire. Most of the wood they did find was either frozen solid or wet. In any case, the smoke rising from a fire would attract unwanted attention. In desperation they melted the frozen food in their mouths or tucked it in an armpit until it was thawed enough to chew.

Merely walking was a hazard; their leather boots froze solid, and there was a real danger that they would break. The constant trading of their uniform buttons for food and shelter also created a problem because their buttonless coats and shirts allowed the icy wind to come in contact with their bare skin. They bitterly regretted discarding their gloves, scarves, and blankets on the night they jumped, but that was all in the past now. They gained some protection from the cold by smearing their faces with fat to prevent frostbite, but it was just marginally effective.

Near the end of the second week they ran out of food altogether; their final trail meal consisted of a sugar cube and a piece of lard for each man. Even worse, they had exhausted their uniform button supply and had nothing with which to barter. They did have rubles, but money was useless in the remote villages they visited. By the end of the second week they were reduced to begging for food and shelter.

As they pushed south they encountered the usual natural obstacles that all escapees face, including rivers too wide to cross and too cold to swim. The creeks were usually frozen solid and easy to walk across, but the ice on the rivers was often too thin to walk on. Their solution was to walk upstream until they found a safe ford. It was a puzzling decision because as a rule, civilization is downriver, and where there is civilization there is usually a river crossing.

The low, rolling hills they tramped over were covered with snow and dotted by large and small villages. There was nothing growing for them to scrounge, such as potatoes or turnips, and there was no wildlife except a few birds that were always in the distance. Unable to live off the land, they were entirely dependent on the villages for food, a situation that made them vulnerable to recapture, robbery, or murder.

At the end of the third week they came to a walled town. This was not just a large village; it was a substantial town with a wall that was obviously meant for defense, suggesting that Chinese soldiers were garrisoned there. And so they were. Bandits were a major problem in that area and to the south, and the garrison was there to control them and to protect the town, which was a major trade center.

The probable presence of soldiers gave them pause. Should they go around the town or go in? They figured that they were far enough away from the Trans-Siberian Railway that they need not worry about running into Russian soldiers, and the Chinese villagers had so far been generally friendly. The clincher was that they could not survive another night in the open. They went in.

They would learn that they had entered the Manchurian walled city of Changchun, a Chinese garrison town on the north bank of the Yitong River 150 miles south of Harbin. Changchun was a major trading center for soybeans, and there had been a large Japanese presence in the city since the end of the Russo-Japanese War. Because of the city's importance as a trade center, the Chinese Eastern Railway line from Harbin to Dalian, China's northernmost warm-water port, had a station at Changchun, and the line from Changchun to Dalian was firmly under Japanese army control.

As a major trade center the town attracted people from a wide area, and that worried Killinger and his three companions. But the advantages to having access to a large population became evident when Cleinow found a Chinese man who spoke Russian. Though there was something about the man they did not like, they needed his help to acquire better clothing, supplies, and directions. The interpreter told them that they were in Changchun, and they were happy to hear that their rubles were good there.[3] Their sense of unease about the Russian-speaking interpreter made them decide to buy whatever they could and leave quickly.

The interpreter led them to shops where they could buy clothing and supplies, and did the bargaining for them. Their distrust of him was beginning to diminish when they saw a column of Chinese soldiers coming toward them. The four Germans looked frantically around for a quick way out of the situation, but their interpreter told them to stay where they were. Since there was no alternative, they stayed put and watched as the column halted right in front of them.

At the center of the column were four men, Asians, trussed up and barefoot. The four men were made to lie on the ground, facedown. A large crowd formed, and people pushed forward to watch. The Germans, who had ringside seats, watched in horror as a soldier went from man to man, strangling each with a piece of cord. The interpreter told the Germans that the four men were bandits who had been captured after robbing a caravan. Soldiers grabbed the four corpses by the wrists, and the column marched off, dragging the bodies along with it.

That demonstration of swift justice, combined with the confirmed presence of Chinese troops in the city and the Germans' distrust of the interpreter, caused them to leave the city immediately. They still had rubles to spend and there were things they still needed, but they were now convinced that the threat of betrayal and arrest was too great. The interpreter agreeably led them to the southern gate and warned them not to go directly south. He told them that the area between Changchun and Mukden was thick with bandits and it would be safer to head toward Kirin, sixty-seven miles east on the Sungari River. The Yitong River was a tributary of the Sungari, so all they needed to do was follow it to the Sungari and then follow that river to Kirin.

The Germans paid the man for his services and thanked him for his help and advice. Because they did not trust him, they told him they were American professors on a walking expedition of northern Asia and that they planned to go west from this point to the Harbin-Mukden rail line.

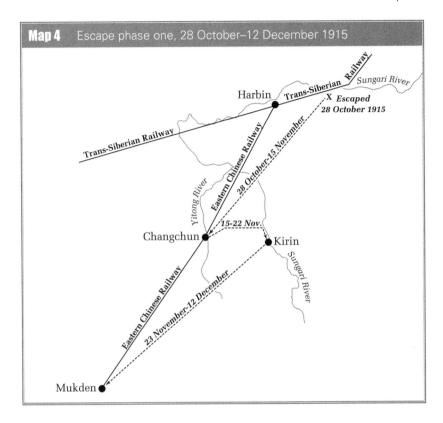

Map 4   Escape phase one, 28 October–12 December 1915

The man probably was not fooled; Changchun was *on* the Harbin-Mukden rail line, and if they were going to walk west to the tracks they had only about a half-mile to go.

After the interpreter disappeared back through the town gate, the four "professors" set off on what they thought was an easterly course toward Kirin, certain that even without a compass they could walk directly to the city. From the time they jumped off the train until they entered Changchun, they had traveled eight to nine miles a day. If they could maintain the same rate, they should reach Kirin in about a week. But their lack of a compass almost proved their undoing; they were walking more north than east. Now that they were more warmly dressed and comfortably fed, they accomplished the first day's walk with little hardship. But that evening, as they stood atop a hill that gave them a panoramic view of the land, they saw smoke from a slow-moving, southbound train and realized that they were looking at the Harbin-Mukden Railway. And it was much too close. If the Japanese or the Russians controlled the line from Harbin to Mukden, then Japanese or Russian troops probably patrolled the tracks. They thought there was a greater possibility that the Japanese controlled that stretch (they did), but that did not diminish their need to get away from there.

They set off at once in the same direction they had been traveling, still thinking that they were headed east. They were in such a panic that they walked throughout the night, stopping only to rest for a few minutes. Based on what happened next, it appears that they actually walked north and a little east, so that instead of getting closer to Kirin they essentially maintained the same distance from the city. At dawn they came to a very wide, very deep, and utterly impassable river that was almost certainly the Yitong. All they had to do at that point was turn right and follow the river to the Sungari, but they did not know that. After losing most of a day trying to find a way across, they came across an elderly man on a donkey, who unintentionally provided the solution to their problem.

The rider was terrified when four wild-looking Germans suddenly surrounded him and started asking questions in a language he had never heard. Panicked, the man kicked his donkey in the ribs, broke away, and headed toward the river as fast as the donkey could go, with the Germans following. The old man went directly to a village on the riverbank and spread the alarm. Whatever the old man told the villagers about the barbarians who had accosted him on the road caused a furor. When the Germans finally plodded into the village, the inhabitants were in an uproar.

The Germans were smart enough to stand in a group and wait quietly for people to settle down before they tried to make actual contact. After the excitement died down, the villagers seemed more afraid of the Germans than hostile and clearly were eager to be rid of them. Just as anxious to go, the Germans pointed to a ferry that was tied up to the riverbank and with gestures indicated that they wanted to go across the river. The village economy was based on the ferry, so the villagers were happy to oblige them—for a price.

The ferry operator was also the village headman, and gesturing toward the ferry he made the international hand sign for payment by holding out his hand, palm up. Lehmann, who was in charge of the Germans' limited cash resources, put a kopek on the open palm. The ferryman shook his head and continued to hold out his hand. The pantomime continued until Lehmann had placed several coins in the man's hand and the ferryman accepted the fee.

Crossing the river turned the page on their bad luck, because on the other side the Germans found a well-used road heading south. A well-used road meant heavy traffic, and in that part of the world heavy traffic meant commerce; and where there was commerce there would be a German consulate. What they had found was the Changchun-Kirin caravan route. After a short hike they entered a village that was a gathering point for carts and wagons joining the caravan to Kirin.

There were two more pleasant discoveries. The first was that Chinese troops did not accompany the convoys; the other was that the convoy had no armed escort because none was needed, a situation that measurably reassured the Germans. They easily found a cart driver who, for their last rubles, agreed to take them to Kirin.

Not long after the caravan got under way, the Germans discovered that riding was not much easier than walking. The cart's motion made them all sick, and they dismounted to walk behind the cart. But walking was not something that they could do for very long because they were nearing the end of their endurance. They were undernourished, badly fatigued, and footsore. Recognizing that motion sickness was the better of the two evils, they climbed back into the cart. Though the cart was uncomfortable, it beat walking. The caravan was eating up the distance at around fifteen miles a day by traveling from sun-up to sunset; a pace that the men could not make on foot.

On the fourth day the caravan entered a village that was garrisoned by Chinese troops and came to a halt, strung out along the main street through town. Soldiers went down the line questioning every cart driver and in some cases searching the carts. The Germans knew that China was a neutral country, but they had no idea how the Chinese soldiers would react to Germans who had escaped from the Russians. Hiding in the cart was not an option; the soldiers would certainly find them, and that would make the situation worse. In the end they decided to take their chances and remain together behind the cart.

Their concern rose when a Chinese colonel questioned their driver. The driver gestured toward the four Germans behind his cart, and the officer approached them. He said something that none of them understood, and when Cleinow responded in Russian the Chinese officer looked blank. Cleinow's use of Russian rather than German might have been behind what happened next. Although the Chinese officer did not seem to understand Russian, he recognized the language and probably thought he was dealing with four Russians, whose presence would not have been remarkable in that area. After another exchange with the driver, the officer turned and called a Chinese soldier over to the cart. There was more conversation, and the soldier climbed into the cart and sat down. The officer motioned the Germans to get into the cart, said something to the driver, and walked away.

Having completed the checkpoint inspection, the caravan again got under way. The four Germans looked at the Chinese soldier, who looked back at them without much interest. What was his assignment? Was he there to keep an eye on them until he turned them in to the Chinese authorities in Kirin? They had no idea and no way of asking him. Finally Killinger gestured that he wanted to look at the man's rifle, and the soldier handed it to him. He examined the rifle, opened the bolt, and saw that there was no round in the chamber. Baffled but reassured, he returned the rifle.

They reached Kirin the next day at about noon, a week after they had walked out of Changchun. This was the largest town they had seen so far, and they correctly assumed that they would find Europeans, including Russians, in the city. Their worries increased when they saw that Chinese soldiers were posted at regular intervals along the streets. They managed to convey to the Chinese soldier riding with them that they needed an interpreter.

The convoy finally reached an open area and stopped. The driver gestured to his passengers to dismount, and the soldier disappeared into the crowd. The Germans spent a nervous thirty minutes waiting until the soldier returned with a Chinese man who spoke some Russian. Once again the task of getting information fell to Cleinow. Using a mixture of gestures and Russian, he learned that there were several Europeans in the city, including French and British legations—and two German businessmen.

They also learned that the Chinese soldier had not been sent along to betray them or even to keep an eye on them. The colonel wanted his wife brought to his garrison and had sent the soldier to fetch her. It cost the officer nothing because the soldier rode in a cart for which the Europeans had already paid. Having found an interpreter for the Germans, the soldier vanished to complete his mission.

A tall, well-dressed European had been closely watching them talking to the interpreter. When it appeared the discussion was drawing to an end, he stepped forward and said something in Russian. It sounded like a question. Before anything else was said, he repeated the question in German, "*Kann ich Ihnen helfen?*" Four golden words: "Can I help you?" He even paid the interpreter before sending him away.

Having introduced himself and shown his good intentions, he hustled the four fugitives out of the square and down a street to his house. Once inside, he bolted the door and told his four guests that they were in great danger in Kirin, and that the interpreter was a known informer. He explained that Kirin was the Manchurian capital and a city of about one million inhabitants. There was a strong Allied presence here, and the Chinese authorities would intern them if they learned that they had escaped from the Russians. He said that six months earlier eleven German and Austrian officers had tried to reach Kirin after escaping from a Russian POW camp. Most of them died along the way, and only four reached Kirin; one of the four died shortly after he arrived. The Chinese arrested the remaining three and interned them in Tientsin.

He explained their situation in grim terms. The interpreter had certainly already informed the Chinese military authorities that there were four Germans in town. The fact that they had arrived in a caravan cart made it obvious that they were escapees. And since there were only two German nationals living in the town, the Chinese would have no difficulty finding the fugitives. On the bright side, their host assured them that they were safe for at least twelve to eighteen hours because the Chinese always conducted searches and raids during the early morning hours. He then offered them dinner.

During dinner, their host told them that they should go to Mukden, where they would find a German consulate. He cautioned them not to go directly to the consulate, because that would draw suspicion to them. Instead, he said, they should ask for directions to the American consulate, which was located right next door.

The four ate well that evening, enjoyed their first baths in several months, and slept comfortably in warm beds. Shortly before dawn a Chinese officer and a squad of soldiers came to the door asking to see the four Germans. The German told the officer that they were not presently in the house but would return around eleven in the morning. That four Germans would be away on some sort of errand when it was still dark outside and the town was asleep apparently failed to arouse any suspicion on the part of the officer, who left.

Knowing that the officer would be back with reinforcements, the German roused his guests and told them they had to leave the city at once. When they were ready, he opened the front door, checked the street in both directions, and motioned his guests to follow him. He took them to the city's south gate and paid the driver of a large freight wagon drawn by eight mules to take them to Mukden, about 215 miles away as the crow flies. He gave each man a small package that included food and cigarettes, and said farewell.

After their hurried departure, the trip settled down to a grinding routine. The wagon's rigid suspension produced a bone-jarring ride on the deeply rutted road, and its cargo left little room to find a comfortable perch. The caravan covered about fourteen or fifteen miles each day between sunrise and sunset, with a midday stop to eat and rest. The greater the distance the caravan put between itself and Kirin, the safer the escapees felt. The biggest threat they faced on this part of the journey was crushing boredom.

On 1 December 1915 they neared the Harbin-Mukden railroad crossing and faced a new threat: the Japanese controlled this part of the line and there was a military checkpoint at the crossing an hour away. The Germans did not know for sure that the crossing was guarded, but they strongly suspected it would be, and they tried to convince their driver to take another route. But the language barrier as well as the fact that the driver was following the known route to Mukden and was part of a caravan nullified their efforts.

There was a hurried debate about what to do. Should they leave the caravan and start south on foot? They rejected that idea for two reasons. First, they were in bandit country, which was the reason the caravan was taking the protected route. Second, they were no longer physically capable of walking to Mukden, which was still a long way off. Their only option was to take their chances at the checkpoint.

When the crossing came into view an hour later, the four Germans did not like what they saw. What appeared to be a full rifle company of Japanese infantry was guarding the approach to the crossing. The bulk of the troops were bivouacked in a field adjacent to the crossing, but two squads of riflemen were formed up on both sides of the road where it crossed the tracks, with an officer standing on one side and a sergeant on the other. The soldiers' rifles were at slung arms with fixed bayonets. The officer and the sergeant were watching the caravan approach, but the Japanese troops were looking straight ahead, seemingly staring at the faces of the men across from them.

As the caravan rolled through the gauntlet between the two lines of infantry, the officer and the sergeant studied the wagons and passengers but made no move to stop or question anyone. The four Germans, on foot, kept close to the cart as they passed between the two lines of soldiers. The Japanese soldiers appeared to stare at them, but that might have been the Germans' imaginations rather than fact. In any event, they passed through the checkpoint without incident.

The remainder of the trip to Mukden was uneventful and followed the usual routine; the caravan traveled until evening and then camped for the night. Apparently the fee for taking them to Mukden included one meal a day, because the driver fed his four passengers every night. There were no morning or midday meals for them. Maintaining their fourteen- to fifteen-mile-a-day pace, they arrived in Mukden on 12 December 1915, twelve days after they had passed through the Japanese checkpoint at the Harbin-Mukden railroad crossing.

THE ESCAPE PIPELINE

12 December 1915–1 January 1916

Six weeks and three days after they jumped from the train, the four escapees made contact with German consular officials in Mukden, who introduced them to the organized German escape system. The German Foreign Office was responsible for maintaining and operating the system wherever there was a German consulate. When Killinger, Brunn, Lehmann, and Cleinow arrived in Mukden, the German escape pipeline was functioning efficiently, though it was certainly not overburdened. It continued to operate until China declared war on Germany in 1917.[1]

The German Foreign Office was responsible for funding, staffing, and operating the escape system because only the Foreign Office had offices and representatives in all parts of the world where Germany had interests. Foreign Office representatives provided escapees with civilian clothes, money, and identity papers, which were usually counterfeit passports, and also arranged for lodging and transportation along the route back to Germany. Each escapee received a "history" to match his new identity and could draw on anyone who was associated with the German embassies and consulates throughout the world for assistance.

The only other German agency involved in the escape system was the Imperial Navy's shadowy intelligence agency subsection, the Etappendienst. The Etappendienst's primary mission was to provide coal, victuals, water, and spare parts to Germany's far-flung ocean raiders. Almost as important was the mission to provide the German war industries with raw materials, especially nickel, tungsten, oil, rubber, cotton, and hemp. A third mission was to gather intelligence on industrial capacity and merchant fleet strength of the world's industrial nations and global traders.

To accomplish those three missions the Etappendienst had established cells called *Etappen* in every major seaport in the world. Each *Etappe* was composed of men who were in some way involved in shipping and the export and import business. Most cell members were either expatriate Germans living in the city where the cell was located or men of German extraction who were citizens of the country in which the cell was located.

Each cell worked closely with the local German embassy or consulate, providing members who could act as guides and provide information useful to the escapees and shelter in a safe house. But their greatest contribution was providing each escapee with the information he needed to find a ship and a captain who would take him on board.

Geography and the distribution of German consulates throughout China made Mukden the first way station for nearly all German and Austrian escapees from Siberia. But simply arriving in Mukden did not mean that the escapees were safe. The Japanese maintained a strong military presence in the city and were suspicious of all Europeans who showed up there. Usually, the Japanese turned over escapees they caught to the Chinese, knowing that the Chinese would intern them. But there was always the possibility that the Japanese might keep a prisoner and ship him to a POW camp in Japan.

Heeding their Kirin host's advice, the Germans avoided suspicion by asking for directions to the American consulate. Once there, they simply walked another three hundred feet to the German consulate and entered. The German clerk who greeted them seemed disinclined to believe that the four tramps standing in front of his desk were really German officers. After a rather heated exchange with the men, the clerk called in another staff member who asked a few questions and immediately ushered the four into another office.

As soon as it became evident that the four men actually were escaped German officers, the situation changed dramatically. The German consul arranged for each of them to be outfitted with civilian clothes and a counterfeit passport. The efficiency of the escape pipeline operation was impressive. Several Chinese tailors arrived to make the new clothes on the spot, and finished them the same day. Equally efficient was the making of four flawless passports, all done in the consulate, complete with current stamps and seals. Killinger and Brunn received American identities, Lehmann was French, and Cleinow was a Swiss missionary.

Passports today are sophisticated documents that are difficult to counterfeit, but in 1915 counterfeiting a passport for any country was fairly easy. Although passports in one form or another had been around for centuries, before World War I they were not universally required for international travel. It was only at the start of World War I that the British first demanded a booklet passport to establish a person's national identity, mainly to prevent German reservists from slipping through the blockade on their way to Germany to join the army. Prior to World War I, passports consisted of a sheet or two of paper with a minimum of information about the holder; papers were usually folded like a letter and kept in an inside coat pocket. After the start of World War I, booklets became the standard passport form, and by 1915 the paper passports had virtually vanished. Nevertheless, the stamps, seals, and banners on passports were easily reproduced.

Along with a passport, the consulate official gave each of the escaped officers fifty Mexican silver dollars. Mexican silver coins were common currency among seamen and merchants in the Far East in the late nineteenth and early twentieth centuries, and the German embassy in Peking and every German consulate in China had a substantial supply on hand.[2] The German navy had been supplying Mexican silver dollars to its gunboats and river gunboats stationed in China for operating expenses since the Germans had occupied Tsingtao in 1897.[3]

Three days after they arrived in Mukden, the consul told them they should leave as soon as possible because the local Russian-language newspapers were reporting that four German POWs were loose in China and headed south. The newspapers provided a description of each man. Since only Killinger and Brunn spoke English, each was paired with one of the non–English speakers, Lehmann and Cleinow, for the trip. Killinger and Cleinow left that day on the evening express to the treaty port of Tientsin, and Brunn and Lehmann followed three days later.

A Chinese driver delivered Killinger and Cleinow to the train station at 9 p.m., and the wisdom of pairing an English speaker with a non–English speaker became immediately evident: they had to arrange for their sleeping car quarters through a British railroad agent. Cleinow waited by the train while Killinger dealt with the matter.

If the Englishman detected Killinger's slight German accent he apparently ignored it. He directed Killinger to place the two names on a sleeping

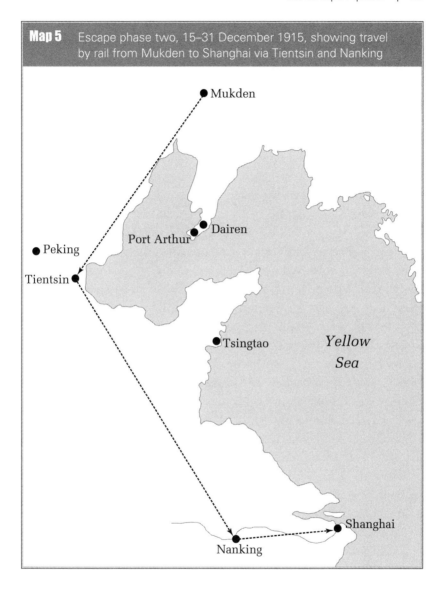

Map 5 Escape phase two, 15–31 December 1915, showing travel by rail from Mukden to Shanghai via Tientsin and Nanking

car roster and did not ask for any identification. Killinger wrote the names under which they were traveling, and the agent gave him two sleeping-car tickets with berth assignments. Killinger returned to Cleinow and gave him his berth assignment, and both men boarded the train thirty minutes before departure.

A very small point, but one that could have revealed Killinger's nationality, was the way he wrote out his and Cleinow's names for the ticket agent. Like all Germans who were trained in cursive before World War I, his handwriting was in *Kurrent*, more commonly called *Kurrentschrift* or *Deutscheschrift*, which was markedly different from the cursive form used by the British and most Americans. Killinger had an excellent education, and it is possible that he was also taught to write in English cursive, and if so, he might have had the presence of mind to use that form when he wrote the names. More likely the ticket agent never looked at the signatures.

When the train came to a halt at 11 p.m. both men were in their bunks, properly dressed in their nightclothes, and feigning sleep. Killinger carefully pulled the window curtain aside and peered out. The train was stopped in a station, and Japanese troops lined the platform facing the train. Killinger quickly closed the curtain and got back into his bunk. A few minutes later he heard voices in the corridor and then a rap on the room door. Killinger answered in English, using his sleepiest, most irritated tone of voice, "Damn it! Go to hell!" There was no response, and whoever it was moved away down the corridor. The train remained in the station for an hour and a half while Killinger and Cleinow lay anxiously awake. After the train got under way again, both men fell into deep sleep. They awoke the following morning to bright sunshine.

Their next hurdle was getting breakfast. Cleinow could not speak English, and speaking in German was not a good idea, so the two decided that Killinger would do all the talking and Cleinow would pretend to be hard of hearing. He would stare out the window most of the time, and if he spoke at all would say, "Very nice," and nod his head. They worked twenty minutes on perfecting "very nice," until Cleinow sounded something like an American, and then went to the dining car.

As they stepped into the dining car the English ticket agent, now in the role of the dining car maître d', came up and asked how they had slept. Killinger gave a short reply, and he and Cleinow took a window table. Cleinow immediately began studying the outside view. Killinger was looking at the menu when a Chinese waiter came to their table and asked them what they would like for breakfast. Killinger ordered for both of them, but the waiter misunderstood and thought Killinger was ordering only for himself and repeated the question to Cleinow. Recognizing that the waiter was speaking to him, Cleinow turned his head toward the waiter, smiled, nodded, and said, "Very nice," then turned back to the window. Killinger quickly jumped in to tell the waiter that they were both having the same thing.

Moments later the ticket agent–*cum*–maître d' returned and asked Cleinow if his ticket was correct. Cleinow had the presence of mind to keep his mouth shut and looked questioningly at Killinger, who leaned toward Cleinow and spoke slowly and in clearly enunciated English, "He wants to know if everything is in order with your ticket." Cleinow immediately realized what was happening, nodded his head, said, "Yes," and turned back toward the window. Killinger explained that his friend was very hard of hearing and that they were both extremely pleased with their accommodations and tickets. The man said nothing more and left, leaving Killinger to wonder nervously why the Englishman was showing such a striking interest in them. They were left alone for the remainder of the trip and arrived in Tientsin the following day at noon.

The German consular representative who had given them their send-off briefing had told them to get off the train in the Chinese station rather than the station in the European section of town. A consular car and official were waiting there for them, but instead of going to the consulate they were driven to the German army barracks in the German concession and housed in the officers' quarters.

Tientsin was an international treaty port with eight foreign concessions—six European, one Japanese, and one American—each fully self-contained with its own schools, barracks, military contingent, jail, and hospital. Treaties of extraterritoriality made each concession an essentially sovereign foreign enclave in the city. Tientsin was both the next way station along the escape route and the main security clearing station at which escapees were vetted before being sent to Shanghai. Whether it was true or not, the Germans believed that British agents were constantly trying to infiltrate the escape system. Based on the low volume of escapee traffic through China, the fear was probably unfounded. Nevertheless, the Germans turned over to the Chinese anyone who failed the vetting.

The procedure in Tientsin was more formal and security much tighter than it had been in Mukden. An officer interrogated them at the military barracks to establish that they actually were escaped military personnel. Typically, escapees had no identification papers with them when they arrived, and the questions centered on aspects of German military service that only a soldier or sailor could answer correctly. In Killinger's case, the interrogator focused on the Marineschule.

That evening, Killinger and Cleinow were introduced to some men who had allegedly escaped before they had and were still in Tientsin before moving down the pipeline. One of these "escapees" was a man from Heidelberg who spoke with Killinger about their hometown and places that both men knew well. Killinger enjoyed the evening and gave his home address to his newfound friend, asking him to contact his parents when he returned to Germany. Killinger did not realize until much later that the escapees were actually garrison officers who were conducting the last part of the vetting process. Killinger and Cleinow passed inspection.

The vetting procedure also included a physical examination by a Chinese doctor, the idea being that an infiltrator would be much too healthy to pass for an escapee from a Siberian POW camp. If poor health evidenced by malnutrition, extreme fatigue, and a bad case of scabies was a measure of a certifiable escapee, Killinger passed with flying colors. An army doctor treated the scabies and gave Killinger a salve to rub on the affected areas.

The next stop after Tientsin was Shanghai, another international treaty port. Instead of occupying individual concessions, however, the foreigners were all gathered in the International Settlement, which was largely run by the British. As in Tientsin, the International Settlement had its own police and fire departments, schools, and hospitals; but in Shanghai the foreign concessions remained Chinese territory. With its numerous nightclubs, cabarets, and fine dining houses, the Shanghai International Settlement had a reputation for extravagance, excess, and wild life. It was a very dangerous place for an escaped POW who was trying to go home.

While still in Tientsin, Killinger became seriously ill with dysentery. The consular representatives immediately called a doctor, who determined that he was too ill to continue the trip to Shanghai. Killinger was put into the German concession's hospital, where he remained for two weeks while Cleinow went on to Shanghai alone. While Killinger was in the hospital, a consulate official visited him, gave him three hundred Mexican silver dollars, and told him that he would receive documents, money, and final instructions for returning to Germany when he reached the German consulate in Shanghai. The official also gave him an assignment.[4]

On his way to Shanghai, Killinger was to make a stop in Nanking to visit the fifty-nine interned crewmen of the German torpedo boat SMS

S-90.[5] The torpedo boat, part of Germany's East Asian Cruiser Squadron based at Tsingtao during the Japanese siege, had torpedoed the Japanese cruiser *Takachiho* on the night of 17 October 1914, sending her to the bottom along with 271 of her 375-man crew. It was the Japanese navy's largest loss of life due to enemy action in World War I. The visit was not a social call. He was to deliver a coded message to *S-90*'s captain, Kapitän-leutnant Paul Brunner. For the purpose of the special side trip the consular official gave Killinger papers identifying him as an American Lutheran missionary.

Without elaborating, the official told him that after he left Tientsin he would make an overnight stop in Nanking and stay in a hotel owned by a German expatriate. In addition to catering to Europeans, the hotel was a safe house for escapees. Unlike many ordinary people who at one time or another worked along the Asian escape route, the German expatriate who ran the hotel knew exactly what he was doing and who his mystery guests were.

Killinger boarded the train for Shanghai on the day he was discharged from the Tientsin hospital and got off a day later in Nanking. He delivered his message to Kapitänleutnant Brunner and went directly to the hotel. The German hotel owner put him in a room with another German who had escaped from a prison train with two other officers several weeks before Killinger and his group made their escape from the train near Harbin. The man had already been to Shanghai and was taking the Asian-European route back to Germany.

The next morning, again traveling as an American citizen, Killinger resumed his journey to Shanghai. Heinrich Baumgartner, a German businessman who was also an Etappendienst cell member, met him at the station and took him to his home in the German district of the International Settlement. Baumgartner's task was to brief Killinger on what he would need to know for his trip home.

First, Baumgartner described the routes Killinger could take to go back to Germany. There were basically two choices: land or sea. The land route, the more commonly used of the two, passed through Russia. An escapee went by ship from Shanghai to Vladivostok, where he took the Trans-Siberian Railway back across Russia to St. Petersburg. From there he went to Stockholm and then into Germany. There was a variation of that route that omitted the sea leg to Vladivostok and went entirely by rail from Shanghai to St. Petersburg.[6]

Several factors made traveling across Russia appear to be the safer route. The most important was the almost universal illiteracy among the Russian enlisted men who manned the various checkpoints and border crossings. Unable to read what was written in the escapee's travel documents, the illiterate soldiers readily accepted the high-quality counterfeits on the basis of their leather bindings and official-looking stamps and seals. The Russian officers' lax attitude toward foreign travelers was another factor in favor of this route. The officers who commanded the checkpoint and border crossing detachments rarely examined the documents at all, and made perfunctory examinations when they did. And luggage was hardly ever opened for inspection. In sum, Russian soldiers rarely bothered an escapee who was properly dressed and equipped with excellent counterfeit documents.

That was all very reassuring to hear, but the fact was that very few escapees from Russian POW camps successfully made the run to Germany on that route. A German cavalry officer, Oberleutnant Paul Freiherr Wolff von und zu Todenwarth, was one of the fortunate few. He escaped in the spring of 1915, used the Asian-European route, and made it back to Germany in July, having traveled on a Norwegian passport even though he spoke absolutely no Norwegian.[7] On the other hand, Oberleutnant Franz von Kochanowski, who spoke Russian fluently and carried impeccable papers, was never heard from again.[8] Brunn, Lehmann, and Cleinow all chose that route, but there is no record that they successfully returned to Germany. Killinger had seen enough of the Trans-Siberian Railway to last him a lifetime, and he rejected the idea immediately.

The second option, the sea route, was extremely dangerous and rarely used. On that route an escapee took a ship to either Nagasaki or Yokohama, then went east across the Pacific to Hawaii, and from there sailed on to San Francisco. The liners that made the trip were either Japanese or American, and it was a matter of which was available that determined which nationality the escapee drew. The nationality of the liner did not really matter, though; the transpacific part of the trip was essentially risk-free if the escapee observed the rules.

Once the escapee reached San Francisco, he took a train to Chicago and then went on to New York. In New York he had to find a ship, usually a neutral-flagged one that would take him to Norway, from where he could enter Germany. And therein lay the danger. Every neutral ship approaching the coast of Europe had to pass through the British blockade. The British intercepted every ship, took it into a port, and sent Royal Navy inspectors on board who thoroughly examined the ship, crew, and passengers.

One of the first to try the route was Oberleutnant zur See Gunther Plüschow, a naval officer who had been a Taube pilot at Tsingtao. He flew his plane out of the colony as the Japanese were entering, landed some distance away, and managed to reach Shanghai. He departed Shanghai en route to San Francisco on 5 December 1914 on the Pacific Mail steamer SS *Mongolian* and then crossed the United States without difficulty, but when his ship put into Gibraltar for inspection, the British grabbed him and sent him to England. He was imprisoned in Donington Hall but managed to escape and get to Germany in July 1915, gaining fame as one of only two German POWs ever to escape from England and return to Germany.

The second was U-Steuermann der Reserve Gustav Völker, the war pilot on the U-12. He was captured together with nine other crewmen and escaped through a tunnel in late September 1915 from a POW camp near Maidenhead. He made his way to Hull, where he signed on the Swedish SS *Ironstorp* as an able seaman. The ship was en route to Kristianstad when the U-16 stopped her in the North Sea and took Völker on board. The U-boat returned him to Germany and he was assigned to the U-44 in January 1916. Völker and the entire crew were lost on 12 August 1917 when the U-44 went down off the coast of Norway.[9]

Next to try the sea route were two Austrian army doctors, Karl Kassowitz and Lothar Ebersberg, who escaped from a POW camp north of Vladivostok on 16 December 1914. At the Austrian embassy in Peking they were outfitted with civilian clothing and issued genuine Austrian passports, dated 14 June 1914, in their own names because the British were at that time allowing civilian medical doctors, regardless of nationality, to pass through the blockade. The two doctors departed Shanghai on the Pacific Mail steamer SS *Manchuria*, crossed the United States by train, and took passage on the Italian passenger-freighter SS *Stampalia* out of Hoboken, New Jersey.

The Royal Navy stopped their ship off the coast of Spain and took her into Gibraltar for inspection. The doctors' cover story was that they had left Austria before the war, as evidenced by their pre-war-dated passports, to work in China. The Royal Navy inspector did not believe they were medical doctors. He believed they were Austrian reservists who had been in China when the war started and were trying to get home to join the Austrian army. A Royal Navy doctor quizzed them briefly and agreed that they were not genuine medical doctors. The two men were confined on Gibraltar for several months before a full medical board determined that they were indeed medical doctors and ordered their release. They got home in December 1915.[10]

Another escapee who chose to try his luck on the ocean route was infantry Oberleutnant Franz Wlad, who sailed out of Shanghai on the Pacific Mail steamer SS *Manchuria* on 26 June 1915, arrived in San Francisco on 21 July, and sailed from Hoboken on board the Scandinavian-American liner SS *Frederik VIII*. One of the Tenth Cruiser Squadron auxiliary cruisers stopped the *Frederik VIII* on 18 August and took her into Kirkwall for inspection. Oberleutnant Wlad spoke Russian fluently and was traveling with authentic-looking Russian papers that identified him as Ivan I. Malysz. Unfortunately for Wlad, the papers had been issued previously to a German army reservist who had used them to return to Germany to fulfill his military obligation. Since a man identified as Ivan I. Malysz had already passed through Kirkwall, the examiner immediately detained Wlad and sent him to a POW camp in England; he was repatriated on 18 May 1919 on medical grounds.[11]

The German Foreign Office had established the China-Japan-USA pipeline based on the incorrect assumption that passing through Japan posed little threat to a properly documented and clothed escapee. The Germans' incorrect assumption stemmed from two widely held views of the Japanese. The first was the unfounded belief that Japan was secretly pro-German; the second was the more accurate view that the Japanese were focused on their war in China rather than on what was happening in Europe and would pay scant attention to Europeans traveling from China to the United States.

The Japanese were indeed focused on their own interests in the Far East to the virtual exclusion of events in Europe, but the Foreign Office overlooked the fact that the Japanese were suspicious of *all* foreigners who entered Japan regardless of whose side they were on. Foreigners passing through Japan on a booked passage to the United States probably received less attention, but if the Japanese suspected that a foreigner was up to something—or was an escaped German officer—they would arrest him at once. Baumgartner emphasized that the best policy for an escapee taking this route was to stay on board while the ship was in Japan.

Once the ship left Japan for the United States Killinger would be in virtually no danger unless he talked too much and raised suspicions about himself among the American passengers. A suspicious American might alert the American authorities that an escaped German was on board, and the Americans would intern him as soon as he landed. But that possibility would be easily avoided if he simply acted like a traveler, stuck to his cover story, and did not become too deeply involved with any of the passengers. Shipboard romances were definitely not encouraged. It was another tiresome warning that Killinger either did not hear or chose to ignore.

The two-day layover in Hawaii would be a vacation during which Killinger would have nothing to fear. Upon arriving in San Francisco, he would contact Kapitänleutnant Walter Sauerbeck, who would outfit him with new travel documents and two hundred dollars in U.S. ten-dollar gold coins. Because the activities of the San Francisco Etappendienst cell had attracted heavy negative press coverage since the start of the war, San Francisco was not the place to tarry. Most escapees headed east on the same day they arrived.[12]

The train trip across the United States would be the safest leg of the trip. When Killinger reached New York he would go first to the offices of the Hamburg-Amerika Line at 45 Broadway where he would be given the names and addresses of people who would provide him with new travel documents. Going afterward to 9 Broadway, he would meet a German naval officer, Zahlmeister (Paymaster) Adolf Reicke, who would give him another two hundred dollars in gold coins.

At that point Killinger would have to make the crucial decision about how he was going to cross the Atlantic. He could book passage on a neutral ship, sign on one as a seaman, or convince a captain to take him on board as a stowaway. If he chose to cross as a passenger, all he had to do was buy a ticket. If he chose to cross as a working crewmember he had to go to the waterfront in New York or New Jersey and buy a set of seaman's papers or have them made by a professional counterfeiter. A set of genuine papers could be purchased in any waterfront dive from some down-and-out seaman. If Killinger decided to stow away with the connivance of a ship's captain, Paymaster Reicke in New York could provide the names of captains who might cooperate.

Regardless of how Killinger chose to cross the Atlantic, the ship he was on would have to pass through a Royal Navy inspection station during which an examiner would question every person on board. Few fugitives made it through the examination. The British often detained people who were not fugitives simply because they doubted the authenticity of their papers. Compared with the Russians, the British were an impassable stone wall.

Having listened to all the pros and cons, Killinger chose the long, dangerous sea route. He never explained why he made that choice, but there are clues. He was conversationally fluent and literate in English and French, skills that offered many opportunities that would be unavailable if he chose to travel through Russia, where he could not read or speak the language. And he was by nature a risk-taker.

Two days after Killinger arrived in Shanghai, Baumgartner sent him to the German consulate to obtain the necessary identification and travel documents. As the hub of the German escape system in China, the Shanghai consulate was fully equipped to create any identity a man needed, including all supporting documentation. His new identity would include the proper clothing, down to the labels; letters from home; business correspondence; and family photos.

The consulate provided Killinger with an impeccable French passport that identified him as Richard du Fais and bore the stamps of the French vice consul in Chefoo. The consulate also supplied him with letters bearing the letterhead of a Swiss manufacturing company, Brown, Boveri, & Cie., with offices in Shanghai and London. The letters were written on genuine company stationery, and with them came equally genuine company catalogs in English, French, Chinese, and Japanese showing the company's lines of electric motors, generators, and turbine engines. He also received photographs of his French family and a recent French-language newspaper that had been published in China. To further enhance this image of a world-traveling French businessman, the consulate issued him luggage plastered with travel stickers bearing the names of hotels in Europe and Asia.

Although the consulate-produced documents were exceptional in their detail, quality, and apparent authenticity, they described a French national who worked for a Swiss manufacturing firm—a French national who in this case had a German accent. Perhaps the consulate officials reasoned that working for a Swiss company might impart a slight German accent to an employee—even though the company was in the French-speaking part of Switzerland and had a French name. Perhaps they just thought the British would be easily fooled. It was a risk Killinger was willing to take.

At Killinger's request, the consulate also provided him with a legitimate set of German identity papers in his own name but omitting any reference to military service. Killinger had a feeling that traveling as a German national and using his own name in the neutral United States might be better than pretending to be a French national who spoke with a German accent. If the U.S. authorities saw through his bogus French identity, they would surely jail him. But if he went as what he was, the Americans might leave him alone. They were, after all, neutral.

Next came a complete wardrobe cut in the French style. Baumgartner arranged for a Chinese tailor from the French quarter to meet him and Killinger in a hotel room the next day for measurements. The meeting took place early in the morning and ended with the tailor promising to return the following morning with three suits, an overcoat, and a dinner jacket. Baumgartner had already arranged to have the necessary "used" clothing complete with laundry marks delivered to his house in the German section of the International Settlement the next day.

In the meantime, the German consulate booked first-class passage for Richard du Fais on the SS *Shinyo Maru*, a Japanese passenger ship carrying mostly American tourists and businessmen who were returning home. The consulate booked first-class passage because Japanese officials paid little attention to wealthy foreigners who were traveling to the United States. Killinger was scheduled to depart in three days, on 1 January 1916, bound for San Francisco with stops in Yokohama and Honolulu.

During the three days before Killinger sailed, Baumgartner, who had business contacts in Japan, gave him advice on how to behave when the ship stopped there. From firsthand experience he knew that the Japanese were extremely suspicious of foreigners and would not hesitate to arrest him if they got a hint that he was an escaped German POW. He completely rejected the official German view that the Japanese were reluctantly allied with Great Britain and were actually pro-German. The report was hogwash, he told Killinger, citing the fact that the Japanese were holding hundreds of German POWs under brutal conditions.

Baumgartner also instructed him in detail about the French consulate in Chefoo where he supposedly had obtained his passport. Killinger studied maps of Chefoo, memorized the names and descriptions of the buildings next to and near the French consulate, and became familiar with the hotels in which he supposedly had stayed. As things turned out, he should have spent his time studying his Brown, Boveri, & Cie. catalogs.

On the evening before his departure Killinger attended a New Year's Eve party at the German consulate, during which he became suspicious of a waiter who seemed to be exhibiting an unusual interest in him. The other Germans' obsessive fear that British and Russian agents were trying to infiltrate the escape system had apparently rubbed off on him, and he convinced himself that the man was a spy. In what he thought was a cleverly concocted ploy to throw off anyone who might be following him, he told fellow partygoers in a loud voice that he was taking the 11 a.m. train to Nanking the next morning for a New Year's Day hunt with members of the interned *S-90* crew.

The following morning he had his luggage taken to the office of the shipping company's agent to be put on board the *Shinyo Maru* and went to the train station dressed in sports attire. Shortly after he arrived at the train station his imagination convinced him he was being followed and he went through the motions of buying a ticket to Nanking. When the Nanking train arrived, he boarded it, passed through the car, got off on the opposite platform, and ducked behind a heavy baggage cart. There he waited until the train was out of the station before he came out of hiding and walked out of the station.

After shaking off what he believed was a Russian or British agent, he walked into a genuine threat of his own making. When he arrived at the dock, a ship's officer was taking tickets at the foot of the gangplank. Killinger stepped up, reached into his coat pocket—and found nothing. He had either lost his ticket or had left it in Baumgartner's home. One can imagine the surge of panic he felt as he went through his pockets while the officer waited.

But luck and the high quality of the German counterfeit French passport saved him. Seeing that the line behind Killinger was growing, the officer decided to speed things up and asked to see just his passport, which Killinger immediately produced. As he handed the man his passport Killinger was sure that he would be found out. Instead of a close scrutiny of the passport followed by questioning, the officer merely matched Killinger's name with the passenger list and motioned him to board.

Killinger boarded the *Shinyo Maru* with about seven hundred Mexican silver dollars in his luggage and two hundred Japanese yen in his wallet; in 1916 that was a lot of money. It was intended to pay his costs along the route to Germany, costs that included transportation, food, lodging, and, if necessary, bribes. He was twenty-two years old, reasonably flush, well dressed, and traveling first class in a crowd of wealthy high rollers, mostly Americans. He had an image to maintain as a successful businessman and world traveler with money to spend. And he spent it. It was a great way to escape.

TRANSPACIFIC

1–25 January 1916

The minute the steward left the cabin, Killinger went to the salon and mingled with the other first-class passengers. The brief outing gave him cause for alarm when he discovered that among the rich passengers were several British men of his own age who were going to England to enlist. He hurriedly returned to his cabin and planned to remain there, emerging only for meals and an occasional breath of fresh air. He also decided to limit his time on deck to the evening hours when there would be fewer people about.[1]

His resolve to remain out of sight lasted only until the ship was under way. Unable to resist the temptation of enjoying the company of others, especially some of the young women he had seen in the salon, he rationalized that he could not remain a recluse for nearly a month without causing suspicion. He was probably right. Carrying a book under his arm and affecting a distant attitude, he made his reconnaissance, ambling through the gaming room and looking around the smoking salon, which seemed to be filled with Americans drinking whisky and playing poker. On the promenade deck he noticed a man who was struggling to communicate with a Japanese deck steward in French and stepped in to help. The deck steward understood English but not French, and Killinger amiably translated the man's fractured French into English. The steward left to get the man what he wanted, and the man believed he had found a friend.

In his enthusiastic thanks to Killinger, and hoping to cement their new friendship, the man used a mixture of Russian and French to explain his inability to speak English. Killinger was alarmed. Obviously the man was a Russian. In the course of the conversation the man asked Killinger if he spoke German, which Killinger denied. Continuing to play his part as a Frenchman, Killinger shook the man's hand warmly, smiled, and said goodbye.

Satisfied that his encounter with the Russian was not going to cause a problem, he resumed his reconnaissance and was shortly approached by a deck steward who asked if he wanted a lounge chair. Killinger did, and one was immediately delivered. The steward told him that this was a good spot to sit because at tea time several "very nice girls" took tea on the deck nearby. The steward walked away, and Killinger settled into his deck chair and waited to see what developed.

At 2 p.m., exactly as the steward had said, several young women showed up and arranged themselves in deck chairs for tea. Killinger silently agreed with the steward that they were "very nice girls." Two of the young women sat next to him, and one asked in English if he was going to San Francisco. He understood her perfectly and could easily have answered her question in English, but this was a good time to establish himself as a Frenchman, and he responded in French. The woman, an American who did not speak French, asked her friend, who did speak French, what Killinger had said. At that point Killinger broke in, affecting what he thought was English with a French accent, and told her in English that he was indeed going to San Francisco.

The afternoon passed pleasantly, and during his conversation with the two Americans he learned that about half the passengers were British and half were American. Most of the British passengers were businessmen and their wives, the girls told him, but there were several young men among them. He already knew about the young men, and the older businessmen were no threat if he stuck to his cover story. The young women also said that in addition to himself there were four other French citizens on board, three women and a man. There were rumors that the other Frenchman was an opium smuggler, and everyone avoided him. Killinger decided that he too would avoid the smuggler.

A steward came up then and offered to arrange his dinner table assignment, and Killinger turned to the young ladies for advice. The two women studied the passenger list and table assignments before suggesting a small table for four that was already occupied by an American couple and an elderly Englishwoman. Killinger, they thought, would be a perfect fit. He agreed and decided to engage in a fairly active social relationship with the

Americans, believing that they would be unlikely to question his French status and detect the deception.

That evening he discovered to his satisfaction that the ladies had made the right table selection for him. His table partners were Thomas Woodfield and his wife, Susan, who was considerably younger than her husband and was about Killinger's age. The Americans were talkative and outgoing. The Englishwoman had little to say and took almost no part in the dinner conversation, which satisfied Killinger.

The Woodfields were returning from their honeymoon in Siberia, where they had visited several POW camps and, according to Thomas Woodfield, had seen German POWs who were starving and sick. What possessed them to visit Siberian POW camps on their honeymoon is a mystery, but Killinger attributed it to the propensity of wealthy Americans to indulge in strange activities. He apparently did not ask the Woodfields how they managed to get that close to the POW camps.

After dinner Thomas Woodfield invited Killinger to join him at the poker table. Killinger knew little about poker, but he felt that refusing the invitation would have been an insult. The smoking salon was crowded, smoke filled, and noisy—conditions that he attributed to the presence of so many Americans—and he was introduced to the American social custom of offering a stranger a drink. He later commented that whenever he was introduced to an American, the first thing the man said was, "Let me buy you a drink."

By the time he and Woodfield sat down to play poker, Killinger was feeling no pain and had made several new friends. The alcohol tempered what would have been a major shock when he learned that the two men sitting across from him were British. But by then nothing like that mattered, and he was enjoying the camaraderie, good cigars, and great booze. The more time he spent with his new friends, the more certain he was that he had made the right decision to take the sea route back to Germany.

Call it beginner's luck, but Killinger won consistently. According to Woodfield, the two Englishmen were just one step short of being professionals, but Killinger won nonetheless. When they finally cashed in for the night, the ersatz French playboy was up one hundred dollars, quite a large sum at that time. During a final round of drinks, Woodfield and the Englishmen introduced Killinger to their fellow travelers as their *good friend* Richard du Fais.

The next day, while he was enjoying the sun in his deck chair, Thomas Woodfield came to him and asked if he played bridge. Killinger said that he did, and Woodfield asked if he would be willing to fill an empty chair that afternoon. He agreed and that afternoon joined a bridge table with Susan Woodfield and two older English ladies. Susan Woodfield was his partner. The game was boring and the conversation mindless, but the situation kept Killinger occupied and out of sight. And Susan Woodfield was a very attractive partner.

It soon became obvious that Woodfield was a heavy gambler and regularly left his wife to her own devices to entertain herself. Bridge was an acceptable pastime, but it could not go on continuously, and Killinger became Susan Woodfield's regular companion away from the bridge table as well. After dinner, Thomas would disappear into the smoking salon, leaving Killinger to take Susan to the nightly dance and back to her cabin. There is nothing in the available material stating that their relationship was anything but a mutually convenient social pairing, but the same material strongly suggests that there was more to it than that. In any event, having Susan Woodfield constantly at his side gave him a favorable notoriety that enhanced his image as a French rake and lover.

The *Shinyo Maru* was scheduled to make three stops in Japan. The first stop was in Nagasaki, where many Japanese passengers disembarked but no new passengers came on board. Since the ship was to remain in Nagasaki for most of the day, some of the first-class passengers went ashore, Killinger among them. The Japanese officer at the passport control station ignored the first-class passengers, and Killinger did not have to show his false passport. Nevertheless, going ashore was risky and not too smart. Baumgartner had warned him to remain on board, and there was also the fact that he had lost his ticket, which could have been his undoing when he tried to return to the ship. His only proof that he was a passenger on the *Shinyo Maru* was his cabin card, which he carried with him. But luck was with him, and the Japanese allowed all the first-class passengers to reembark without being questioned.

The second stop was in Kobe, where the ship remained for just a few hours. The weather was overcast with occasional rain showers, and this time Killinger remained on board. So did most of the other first-class passengers, who organized an afternoon dance party. Again Thomas

Woodfield disappeared into the smoking salon while Erich and Susan danced the afternoon away. He was having the time of his life escaping, but he was also routinely breaking a rule that Baumgartner had said he must never break.

Baumgartner had emphatically told him to maintain a low profile and not to become involved with the other passengers, especially young women. But by the time the ship reached Kobe, Killinger's profile was anything but low, and he had developed a reputation among the first-class passengers as something of a French blade. That might have been a good thing because he certainly fit in with the crowd, and so far no one seemed to suspect him of being other than what he claimed, least of all that he was an escaped German officer. Had he kept reminding himself who and what he really was, there might not have been a problem, but the more he relaxed his guard and got away with it, the bolder he became.

The third stop was a four-day layover in Yokohama during which all the first-class passengers went ashore to stay in a luxury hotel. Killinger went too because remaining on board would have attracted undue attention, which could become suspicion. He spent four days shopping in Yokohama by day and hitting the hot spots by night. He spent a large sum on Japanese silk, which he bought by the bolt, and clothes. The heavy spending gave him status among his fellow passengers as a very successful young businessman, but it also depleted his cash resources. By the time he returned to the ship, his financial state was becoming precarious.[2]

The *Shinyo Maru* departed Yokohama for Honolulu on 12 January 1916, and during this leg of the trip Killinger made his biggest blunder yet. Convinced that he would need help getting from San Francisco to New York, he confided in Thomas Woodfield his true identity. Woodfield declared himself a Germanophile, readily agreed to help in any way he could, and swore himself to secrecy—and immediately told his wife.

Telling Woodfield was an incredibly stupid thing to do—and completely unnecessary. A consulate official in Shanghai had told him to contact Kapitänleutnant Sauerbeck at the German consulate in San Francisco, who would see to all his needs. Killinger had already experienced the smooth, efficient escape operation during his passage through China, so there was no need for him to drum up his own help. Professional help was already in place, and he knew it.

The first indication that his indiscretion might be catastrophic came the following morning at the breakfast table. When the Woodfields came into the dining salon, Susan rushed up to Killinger, gripped his hand, and gushed, "You are the greatest hero I ever saw in my life." Other passengers within hearing looked at him, wondering what the French playboy had done this time. The immediate result of his indiscretion was that he could never let Susan Woodfield out of his sight for fear that she would say something about him to another passenger. That was easily accomplished because Susan Woodfield rarely left his side for the remainder of the trip.

The ship reached Honolulu and remained there for two days discharging cargo and passengers and taking on new cargo and passengers. Among the new passengers were Mr. and Mrs. J. Fred Havey of Lowell, Massachusetts. Fred Havey was a salesman for Saco-Lowell Shops, one the biggest textile machine manufacturers in the United States. He handled sales in China and Japan through Saco-Lowell's agent, Anderson, Meyer, and Company, in Shanghai. The Haveys had been vacationing in Hawaii and were returning home to Boston. Mr. Havey was about to give Killinger a nasty fright.

While the Haveys were settling in on the *Shinyo Maru*, Killinger and several other first-class passengers took the opportunity to visit SMS *Geier*. The *Geier* was an obsolete light cruiser that had been assigned to the German East Asia Squadron in 1914, but the war broke out before she could reach the German naval base at Tsingtao. Lacking sufficient coal for the return trip to Germany, and unable to re-coal in the Pacific, the captain decided to have his ship interned in Hawaii. Prior to America's entry into World War I, the *Geier's* 165-man crew enjoyed a relatively easy internment in Honolulu, where they were allowed access to the city and the beaches.

The Germans gave the *Shinyo Maru's* first-class passengers a tour of the ship, during which Killinger slipped away from the group and made contact with the *Geier's* captain, Korvettenkapitän Carl Grasshoff. Eager to return to the group before he was missed, he arranged to meet Grasshoff that night in the captain's quarters ashore. During their conversation that evening, Grasshoff gave Killinger the names of two *Geier* officers who could help him once he reached the United States: the *Geier's* navigation officer, Kapitänleutnant Walter Sauerbeck, who was now on Korvettenkapitän Wolfram von Knorr's Etappendienst staff in San Francisco, and the torpedo officer, Leutnant zur See Heinz Panke, who had the same position in New York. Not knowing what their real duties would be, the Americans had allowed both officers to join the consular staffs in those cities after the *Geier* had been interned.[3] Killinger already knew about Sauerbeck, but Panke's name was new to him.

The *Shinyo Maru* departed Honolulu the next day at midnight on the final leg to San Francisco, and the passengers settled back into the ship's routine. Killinger stayed close to Susan Woodfield and remained an active member of the ship's social elite. He put himself squarely at the center of attention when he took part in two inane contests, a pillow fight and a game called "Are you there, Bill?"

The pillow fight involved two contestants astride parallel varnished spars placed an arm's length apart with bath towel "saddles." Each man was armed with a pillow with which he tried to unseat his opponent. The slick varnish on the spar combined with the unsecured bath towel saddle made remaining astride the spar a contest in itself. At the count, both opponents started slapping at each other with their pillows, each trying to knock the other off his spar. Given the slippery spar and towel saddle, the fights were usually very short. Killinger's long arms and his youth gave him an advantage that he used to best all comers until he ran out of male passenger opponents. His last opponent was a ship's officer who swept Killinger off his spar in short order. It was all good fun, and the games committee, composed entirely of American male passengers, awarded Killinger the prize on the grounds that the Japanese officer was disqualified for not being a passenger.

As inane as the pillow fights were, the next game literally took the cake. In this contest, two men were blindfolded and made to lie down on a mattress side-by-side and about an arm's length apart. Each was armed with a rolled-up newspaper and had a piece of frosted cake bound to his forehead with a ribbon. At the command, the first contestant called, "Are you there, Bill?" When the other said, "Yes," the first contestant tried to smash the cake on his opponent's forehead. It was somewhat reminiscent of the swimming pool game "Marco Polo," but much messier. The exchange went on until one of them got lucky. Again Killinger came out the grand winner. Being as visible as he was, he inevitably attracted the attention of J. Fred Havey. Their first meeting took place three days out of Honolulu at the evening meal.

Havey approached him at the dinner table just as the dishes were being cleared away. The elderly Englishwoman had excused herself, and Thomas Woodfield had gone to the smoking salon, leaving Susan Woodfield and Killinger alone at the table. Havey introduced himself as the sales agent for Saco-Lowell Shops in China and Japan, and Killinger, always socially correct, invited him to take one of the empty chairs.

When Havey sat down to chat, he had no suspicions about Killinger's real identity. Havey was merely concerned that "Richard du Fais" might be a competitor in machine sales to China. He was particularly interested in learning who the Frenchman's business allies in China were, and he asked him about several specific Chinese and Japanese companies. A major shortfall in Killinger's preparation for his role now came to light. The Shanghai consulate and Heinrich Baumgartner had thought of everything—except drilling Killinger on details about his employment with Brown, Boveri, & Cie. For his part, Killinger had paid little or no attention to the sales brochures and catalogs that would have made it obvious that he and Havey would have had no contacts in common. Had he been drilled on his cover story or read the material given to him, he could easily have deflected Havey's questions by telling him that Brown, Boveri, & Cie. manufactured marine electric motors, steam and gas turbines, generators, and transformers, and could have explained that his business contacts were all in the maritime industry and had nothing to do with textiles.

But Killinger had never heard of the companies Havey was asking about and was even more ignorant about what it was he himself was supposed to be selling. He tried to evade the questions with vague answers. Havey might have been initially fooled into thinking that Killinger was being cagey and withholding information to protect his interests, but that belief would quickly have been dispelled when the conversation turned to machinery-related issues, such as use and purpose, and it became obvious that the alleged Frenchman was a fraud.

Killinger recognized that he was in trouble when Havey's demeanor changed from interested and friendly to slightly hostile and suspicious. Knowing that he could not duck this issue, he decided to address it directly and invited Havey to his cabin for a private business discussion. Havey's curiosity got the better of him and he accepted. When Killinger was alone with Havey, he appealed to the American's honesty and asked him to keep the secret that he was about to hear. He told Havey that he was a German naval officer who had escaped from the Russians and was trying to return to Germany.

To Killinger's consternation, Havey accused him of being a German spy going to the United States to sabotage American munitions plants. Indeed, in the summer of 1915 a German, Kapitänleutnant Franz von Rintelen, had been responsible for a wave of mysterious fires and explosions in American munitions and powder factories. Havey turned toward the door, telling Killinger that he was going to report him to the ship's captain. Killinger quickly blocked the door with his body. Killinger was six feet, three inches tall, and though he was built like a string bean, he was younger and stronger than Havey. At that moment Havey feared that Killinger was going to kill him and threatened to call out for help if he did not immediately step aside. But Killinger did not step aside, instead pleading his case quickly and with passion. He told the American in fluent English that he meant him no harm and begged him to listen. He described in detail his escape from a Russian POW train and the several-hundred-mile trek through China to Shanghai. He had no intention of attacking any American munitions plants, he insisted. All he wanted to do was get to New York and board a ship for Germany.

At first Havey remained disbelieving, but as Killinger poured out specific details about his escape, including how he had acquired false identity papers, Havey slowly changed his mind. Finally, Killinger appealed to the American's honor, pointing out that the United States and Germany were not at war. That point seemed to register most with Havey. What he wanted from Killinger was assurance that he had no hostile intentions toward the United States, and Killinger swore it on his honor as a German officer. Such an assurance might not carry much weight today, but in 1916 it had the authority of a blood oath, and Havey accepted it.

That evening at dinner Havey explained to the Woodfields that Killinger's seemingly strange and apparently confused answers to his questions were because he believed that Havey was a competitor and was afraid he would divulge business secrets if he answered directly. Since the Woodfields already knew Killinger's secret, they just listened and nodded.

Killinger became increasingly nervous when it became apparent that the Woodfields were talking about him to the other passengers. Which of the two had the flapping lip he never found out, but he suspected them both. On the other hand, the leak might have been Havey. More and more Killinger rued the day that he spilled the beans to Woodfield, although telling Havey was an act of necessity. The revelation that more people than just the Woodfields and Havey knew about his true identity came when the ship was a day out of San Francisco.

A second-class passenger who had slipped through the barrier between the second- and first-class decks approached him in the early afternoon and said that he had to speak with him. Startled but curious, Killinger agreed and took the man to his cabin. The man said nothing while they were walking to Killinger's cabin; once inside he quickly locked the door. Speaking in German, the stranger told Killinger that he knew he was a German officer and that he had often seen him in Shanghai. He said his name was Teplitzki and that he was an ethnic German with Russian citizenship and had fought at the front. He and ten other ethnic Germans had deserted and fled to China, hoping to find passage to the United States. Their goal, he said, was to find work there because they believed that the pay was very high and the Russians would not find them.

The group had dwindled to two, and both were on the *Shinyo Maru* in second class, but their goal had changed. Instead of seeking work in the United States, they were now eager to go to Germany to find work among their ethnic kinsmen. Since he knew that Killinger was also going to Germany, he and his companion wanted to tag along, taking advantage of Killinger's superior knowledge of how to evade capture.

The man's story certainly sounded farfetched, but in fact it was little different from Killinger's own experience in escaping from Siberia through China. Whether the story was true or not, Killinger had to assume that he was a Russian agent intent on penetrating the escape pipeline. But he knew better than to flatly reject Teplitzki, who would have nothing to lose by reporting him to the captain. Instead, he adopted an interested and sympathetic demeanor. He explained that a person who spoke only Russian and German would never slip through the British blockade. And even if he did, the Germans would certainly refuse him entry into Germany. But he did not turn the man away. He left open the possibility of providing assistance when they reached San Francisco, and to show good faith he gave the man a ten-dollar gold coin, implying that there would be more funds available in San Francisco.

Seemingly satisfied with the outcome of their conversation, Teplitzki left the cabin. Killinger was not sure what to think. Was it possible that Teplitzki had gotten on to him in Shanghai, or did he pick up the scent as a result of the Woodfields' loose tongues? And who else knew about him? In any event, he knew that he had to get off the ship quickly in San Francisco and be off the dock before Teplitzki disembarked. He made up his mind to be the first person down the gangplank in the morning.

TRANSCONTINENTAL USA

30 January–9 February 1916

As the *Shinyo Maru* approached the Golden Gate, most of the first-class passengers were on deck to watch the ship enter San Francisco Bay. Fred Havey and Killinger were standing together, leaning on the starboard rail as the liner slid by the Mile Rocks Lighthouse. Both were warmly dressed. Killinger reached into the inside pocket of his overcoat and took out his German passport, which he gave to Havey for safekeeping. Killinger was going ashore as du Fais and was worried that the U.S. authorities would search him. If they did, he did not want them to find the German passport and realize that his French identity was fraudulent. Havey thought that Killinger was being paranoid, but took the papers anyway.[1]

Thirty minutes later the ship was approaching her berth, and Killinger and Havey turned from the rail and went down to the disembarkation deck, planning to be the first off the ship. It was still dark when the *Shinyo Maru* docked at Pier 4, just south of Market Street on San Francisco's Embarcadero waterfront, and Killinger's plan to slip discreetly off the ship was about to explode. His friends the Woodfields were well known in San Francisco, and news of their arrival had been telegraphed to the newspapers while the ship was still at sea. Their Siberian honeymoon was big news among the society set, and a horde of reporters and cameramen were waiting inside the Pier 4 warehouse to interview them.

The first-class gangplank was in place at 6:15 a.m., and Killinger was the first one down it, with Havey right behind. Quickly crossing the narrow walkway between the ship and the building, they entered a cavernous warehouse and hurried toward the customs area. Other eager passengers pushed up behind them, and the brightly lighted hall was rapidly filling. As the crowd grew, Havey and Killinger became separated. Teams of baggage handlers were already dumping first-class luggage in front of the customs area, where a crew of African American baggage handlers quickly moved it onto the customs tables for inspection. The other side of the customs hall was packed with people who were there to meet the returning travelers, and a noisy press group was effectively blocking the exit from customs.

Suddenly discovering that Havey was no longer with him, Killinger looked hurriedly around him, but all he saw were passengers pressing forward to escape the bedlam and get outside. He handed his French passport to a customs agent, who barely looked at it before handing it back with a smile and a greeting, "Welcome to the United States Mr. du Fais." The government official was already reaching for the next passenger's papers as Killinger stepped out of the customs area and plunged into the crowd. He came to an abrupt halt four feet away from an army of reporters and cameramen jostling to get the best advantage. Looking to his left, hoping to find a way through the mob, he came face-to-face with the Woodfields, both of whom breezed past him as they happily pushed toward the press. The reporters responded with a forward surge that almost knocked Killinger off his feet. At that moment the crowd parted slightly in front of him, and he plowed into the hole like a fullback going for yardage.

As he was trying to force his way through the press, he heard Woodfield tell the reporters, "Talk to that man over there," pointing at Killinger. "He is an escaped German officer and can tell you many things about Siberia." In that moment Killinger would have happily killed him. Instead he grabbed the man in front of him by the right shoulder, rudely jerked him out of the way, and charged through the opening. He popped out into the open space behind the crowd and looked quickly for his luggage. No one followed him. He spotted the baggage being stacked thirty feet away and started to head that way, hoping to find Havey already there. But there was a growing clamor to his right as reporters and cameramen tried to push through the crowd toward him. He immediately abandoned any thought of retrieving his luggage and strode through the front entrance onto the Embarcadero. He was not quick enough.

The reporters were on him in a flash, shoving one another to get closer to him. Those who have been subjected to a "press feeding frenzy" will recognize that nothing has changed in one hundred years. Killinger described the scene this way:

One insisted on photographing me and offered me five hundred dollars; another wanted a short statement and offered me more. Every one of them pushed and pulled trying to get me off into a corner where he could talk to me alone. Someone grabbed my arm and others grabbed my coat and started jerking so that I thought they would rip it from my body. I slammed my open hand into one man's chest and that helped, but only for a moment; at least no one laid a hand on me again. I kept insisting I was French and had never spent a day of my life in Siberia. They laughed and told me they had no intention of fooling around any longer; I had to give them a story. One tried to snap a picture, and I tore the camera from his hands and smashed it on the floor.[2]

At that point help in the form of private security police arrived. The reporters' attention was abruptly diverted from Killinger when six burly, uniformed thugs started grabbing shoulders and pulling reporters out of the crowd. The reporters fought back, cameramen started snapping pictures of the melee, and everyone was shouting and shoving. In the noise and confusion Killinger broke away and ran toward a taxi.

Safe in the cab, or so he thought, he told the driver to get away from the terminal as quickly as possible. Before the driver could even shift gears a reporter tried to climb into the cab. Killinger pushed the man out the door as the cab pulled away from the curb, leaving the reporter sprawled on the sidewalk. He still was not in the clear. Several reporters had also grabbed cabs, and the pursuit was on.

Even in 1916 there were traffic signals on some of San Francisco's downtown streets, and one of them changed to STOP as the cab driver headed down Market Street. The press cars immediately pulled up alongside the cab with the reporters shouting through open windows at Killinger. He was again offered five hundred dollars for even a short statement. The signal changed, and the chase continued. Several blocks later the driver made a right turn onto Montgomery with the press still hot on his tail. As he was approaching the intersection at Pine, the cabbie saw the green GO arm start to drop and floored the accelerator. The cab roared through the intersection as the red STOP arm was coming up. The press cars were too far behind to make it. Killinger told the driver to turn right and stop. The cabbie whipped the car onto California and slammed on the brakes. Killinger tossed him a five-dollar bill, hopped out of the cab, and ducked quickly into a doorway. He pressed himself against the door to remain out of sight and watched the press posse speed by in hot pursuit of the now empty cab. Not long afterward, a cab came along and he hailed it, telling the driver to take him to the German consulate.

At ten in the morning on Sunday, 31 January 1915, Killinger entered the German consulate and was immediately taken to Kapitänleutnant Sauerbeck, who was expecting him. The German consulate in Honolulu had telegraphed ahead that Killinger would arrive that day on the *Shinyo Maru*. Sauerbeck gave Killinger a briefing that included what to do when he arrived in Chicago and New York, suggested how best to deal with Americans, and filled him in on the latest war news. Killinger told Sauerbeck that his luggage was still at Pier 4 but added that Fred Havey, who was staying at the St. Francis Hotel, might be able to pick it up. He did not tell Sauerbeck that he had divulged his identity to Havey and the Woodfields.

He had looked forward to spending a couple of days in San Francisco while Kapitänleutnant Sauerbeck arranged his trip across the United States, but that was not to be. That afternoon a special edition hit the newsstands announcing in bold headlines that an escaped German naval officer had arrived on the *Shinyo Maru*:[3]

GERMAN OFFICER ESCAPES FROM SIBERIA
HORROR IN SIBERIA
MR. AND MRS. WOODFIELDS' HONEYMOON TRIP TO SIBERIA

Once again Killinger must have rued the day he took Woodfield into his confidence and wondered if this publicity was what Woodfield had meant when he promised to do anything in his power to help. The article on Killinger, which came entirely from statements Thomas Woodfield had made to the reporter, stated that he was traveling under a false passport in the name of Richard du Fais and that he was a naval aviator, but incorrectly described him as a pilot. The public disclosure meant that he had to assume a new identity and get out of San Francisco quickly.

The German consul was already at work preparing identity papers that described him as Carl H. Frank, a German American, because German Americans were common in America and would not attract any special attention. Kapitänleutnant Sauerbeck gave "Mr. Frank" two hundred dollars in ten-dollar gold coins and the name of the consular agent in Chicago.

Killinger's next stop was the Santa Fe Railroad office at 673 Market Street, where he bought a one-way ticket to Chicago on the *California Limited*. He sent a messenger to Havey at the St. Francis Hotel asking him to arrange to pick up Killinger's luggage at the dock and deliver it to the Santa Fe ferry gate in the San Francisco Ferry Terminal before 5 p.m. The ferry was scheduled to depart the terminal at 6 p.m. and arrive at the Point Richmond Terminal across San Francisco Bay at 7:45 p.m. His train would pull out of the Richmond station at 8:30 p.m. on the dot.

Killinger was about to embark on a cross-continental trip on two of America's premier trains—a trip so luxurious that he later found it hard to describe. He would dine that evening on board the Santa Fe passenger ferry SS *San Pedro* in a Fred Harvey Company restaurant that served excellent steaks in posh surroundings. He would find the same dining facilities on the train. After an overnight leg to Los Angeles, he would remain on the train for another sixty-eight hours before arriving in Chicago, where he would take a cab to Chicago's LaSalle Street Station and board New York Central Railroad's *Twentieth Century Limited*.[4]

Santa Fe's *California Limited,* known as the "finest train west of Chicago," carried only first-class passengers and made only two stops after leaving Los Angeles: one at Williams, Arizona, for passengers going to or coming from the Grand Canyon, and the other at Kansas City, Missouri. The Pullman sleeping cars offered suites with parlors, and the train had a beauty salon, a barbershop, two bar cars, a lounge car, a parlor car, and an observation car. But the crown jewel was the train's elegant dining car, a fully appointed Fred Harvey restaurant where passengers feasted on excellent food ranging from Kansas City steaks to Long Island roast duckling. But the feature that set a Fred Harvey restaurant apart from all others, whether on a train, in a hotel, or as a standalone restaurant, was the serving staff known as the "Harvey Girls."

Harvey Girls were "attractive and intelligent," single, eighteen to thirty years old, white, well mannered, and educated. They wore starched black-and-white uniforms with a modest hemline, an immaculate white pinafore apron, opaque black stockings, and black shoes. The girls were closely chaperoned by the senior Harvey Girl on board, and curfew was 10 p.m.[5]

Killinger had never experienced such luxurious train travel:

> Our largest and best trains in Europe are nothing compared
> to the luxury trains in America. I had a real apartment with

a black servant for me alone. My bedroom was in minutes converted into a homey room. Right next door was a comfortable bathroom with a large bathtub and a shower. The dining car served anything imaginable. There was a reading and smoking car in which you could dictate to a professional typist without cost, which made it possible for American businessmen to continue their work without interruption while traveling. These trains do not stop for water, which accounts for the phenomenal speed with which they cross America. This is possible because every hundred kilometers there is between the tracks a long, water-filled trough called a "track pan" into which the locomotive lowers a scoop as it speeds down the track. Water is forced up through the scoop pipe and into the water tanks in the tender.[6]

He marveled at the ease with which a person like himself could move about the vast country without being questioned. At no time during his trip across America did he have to produce any identification. His experience crossing America caused him to momentarily forget why he was making the trip.

Killinger left the *California Limited* in Chicago, where another consular official took him to a hotel for the night. The next morning over breakfast the official handed him a French passport for Jean DuBois. He also gave him a packet of personal correspondence addressed to Jean DuBois and a new first-class ticket on the *Twentieth Century Limited*, which would leave the LaSalle Street Station that afternoon at 12:30 and would arrive in New York City's Grand Central Station the following morning at 9:30. He was to go directly to the offices of the Hamburg-Amerika Line at 45 Broadway, where he would meet with Paymaster Adolf Reicke. Killinger recognized the name because the consular official in Shanghai had given him the same directions.

The relatively short trip from Chicago to New York was another awe-inspiring experience for Killinger. As posh as the *California Limited* was, it paled in comparison with the New York Central Railroad's premier passenger train. The *Twentieth Century Limited*, at the time the fastest train in America, was famous for its understated elegance and "Red Carpet Service."

Fähnrich zur See Erich Killinger was assigned to the school
cruiser SMS *Vineta* in 1913.

Killinger's first wartime assignment was a light cruiser, SMS *Berlin*,
which was commissioned in 1905 and was obsolescent by 1914.

Killinger in his Jean Epars waterfront-tough disguise

Killinger as a recently promoted Leutnant zur See, March 1916

Officer prisoners were allowed to take walks in the countryside around
Auswertestelle West. One or two German officers accompanied
them, but there were no armed guards.

Oberstleutnant Killinger and an unnamed camp officer in an
undated photo taken at Auswertestelle West

The train arrived in Grand Central Station right on time, and Killinger stepped off the train and into a world he had never imagined possible. He did not go directly to the Hamburg-Amerika Line office on Broadway and meet with Paymaster Reicke. Instead, he checked into the Biltmore Hotel at 335 Madison Avenue and set out to see the sights. Why not? He was twenty-two years old and had money to spend. And what better time to spend it? He would face great peril on the next phase of his trip.

He spent four days being a tourist: riding the subway, enjoying the nightlife, and dining in fine restaurants. His stay in New York City convinced him that Americans lived life at a frantic pace. His visit to the New York Stock Exchange underscored that observation: "As a German, I was astounded by the wild gyrations, arm flailing, and shouting that those people did. The noise was indescribable. People ran to and fro, bells rang, and at times it seemed they were about to riot. The floor was covered with litter that constantly grew because they simply threw whatever was in their hands on the floor."[7]

Despite the fun of being a tourist he still had to get back to Germany and the war. After his four-day spree, he reported to the offices of the Hamburg-Amerika Line for instructions and help. Paymaster Reicke was a German naval officer who took his orders from the German consulate in New York while working in the New York office of Hamburg-Amerika as the line's civilian paymaster, Herr Reicke. Killinger's experience with the Foreign Office pipeline in New York was considerably different from the coddling on the earlier stages of the trip. New York was essentially the end of the line where he was "spit out" and left to his own devices. In San Francisco the Etappendienst had seen to Killinger's needs and prepared him for the next step. New York was another matter.

When Killinger finally reported, Reicke did not ask why he was late. He simply gave him another two hundred dollars in ten-dollar gold coins along with seals from different foreign consulates and two addresses where he could buy a counterfeit passport. There was no offer of a high-quality counterfeit passport from the German consulate, no directions on what he should do next, and no briefing on what to expect when he passed through the British blockade.

One address Reicke gave him was in New York; the other was in Baltimore. The men at both addresses were professional counterfeiters and forgers to whom Reicke was just another customer. Either of them could provide Killinger with a genuine blank passport for fifty to one hundred dollars; but that was just for the blank passport. He had to provide a photo and one of the seals, which the counterfeiter would place on the photograph using the hectograph method. The counterfeiter would also correctly affix the photo in the blank passport and fill in the particulars such as Killinger's assumed name and his physical description.[8]

Killinger still had to decide whether he would cross the Atlantic as a ticketed passenger, a crewmember, or a stowaway under the captain's care. In addition to the counterfeiters' addresses Reicke gave him a list of ships and captains who might cooperate with either of the last two methods. The procedure was to first contact a captain and enlist his aid—buy it if necessary. Many captains would be reluctant. The risk was enormous, and if the British did not accept Killinger's papers, whether he was a crewmember or a stowaway, they could, and probably would, seize the ship and her cargo.

If he chose to travel as a crewmember he would need to buy a seaman's personal papers. Those were available in any waterfront bar, but he had to be sure that they had belonged to a man who resembled him physically. It would not do the six-foot-three Killinger any good to have papers describing him as five-foot-nine. Reicke cautioned him to be very careful when he paid for the papers because if any of the rough sorts who frequented those bars got wind of the amount of money he was carrying, they would rob and kill him. And he would have to buy the papers before buying the blank passport, because the two documents would have to match.

There was an important consideration that would affect what Killinger did regardless of whether he traveled as a passenger or a crewmember. As a matter of policy, the British detained for further investigation any male who was traveling with papers that identified him as Norwegian, Danish, Swedish, or Swiss. That policy dramatically reduced the options open to him, but there was no way around it.

All things considered, posing as a ticketed passenger rather than a crewmember would seem to be the better choice. But he was starting to run low on cash, and even a second-class ticket would cost nearly all he had left. And he believed that the British would look more closely at a passenger than they would at a crewman. In that he was wrong—the British put everybody under a microscope.

Having given Killinger instructions, the paymaster gave him the address of a rundown hotel in Hoboken where he was to meet another agent identified only as Mr. Peters, who would arrange for his lodging. Mr. Peters was actually Leutnant zur See Heinz Panke, the *Geier*'s former torpedo officer. Panke had already gotten him a room and a German-American roommate.

Operating from the hotel, Killinger spent his days hanging around the waterfront getting the lay of the land. He picked up odd jobs chipping paint and loading cargo, which gave him a small income and introduced him to a waterfront character who said he could get anything—for a price. Without giving any reason, he asked the man if he could supply him with a set of legitimate seaman's papers. The man said he could, but they would cost Killinger one hundred dollars. Killinger agreed, and the man arranged a meeting for the following night. The man selling the papers demanded payment in advance, but Killinger held back and negotiated the price down to fifty dollars. The man accepted the offer but still wanted the money up front.

Killinger took the money from his boot, and the man immediately stuck out his hand to take it. Killinger held onto his money and demanded the papers first. They appeared to be at an impasse, and Killinger, believing that the man had no papers to sell, abruptly turned to leave. The man produced the papers, Killinger handed over the money, and the two men went their separate ways. Killinger returned to his room and examined the papers for the first time. They were genuine but worthless. The former owner was fifteen years older than he, and the physical description on the papers was that of a much smaller man.

He had learned a valuable lesson. Rather than spend his time in a futile search for the right papers, he decided to contact the forger at the New York address Reicke had given him. The forger worked out of a basement near the waterfront, and he told Killinger that in addition to a passport he could produce a set of seaman's papers that would fool anyone. But it would cost more money, and Killinger was nearly broke. Having no other choice, he agreed and paid out almost all his remaining cash for a set of counterfeit seaman's papers.

He had decided to be a Frenchman again, but the forger told him that would be a mistake because the British would send him to France to fulfill his military obligation to the Republic. Though Killinger's English was excellent, he knew he could never pass as an Englishman because his German accent would never get past a British inspection officer. That left him no choice but to adopt an identity that would allow him to use his French language ability without being a Frenchman. He chose to become a French Swiss national with the name Jean Epars. The choice of name was no random decision. He knew Jean Epars.

Before the war, he had frequently visited Switzerland to improve his French and to hike in the mountains. There he met and became friends with Pastor Epars, who had a son, Jean, who was three years older than Killinger. The age difference was insignificant, and he had the forger produce a passport that identified him as Jean Epars. At the same time Killinger sent a letter to his sister in Heidelberg telling her to go to Switzerland and visit Pastor Epars. She was to tell him what was happening and ask him to confirm that Jean Epars was his son if anyone asked.

There was no guarantee that his sister would receive the letter; and if she did, Killinger would not know it. He would be at sea before a return letter from her could reach him in the United States. The letter was a shot in the dark, but it was the best he could do under the circumstances to give himself a slight edge. In 1916, sending a letter to his sister in Germany was both a waste of effort and dangerous. One of the major complaints the U.S. Department of State made regularly to the British was about the British policy of not allowing any correspondence to reach Germany. Any mail addressed to a German address—letters and packages—was seized; the packages were opened for inspection and some letters were read.

He knew that his German accent, slight though it was, would be a problem, but he felt that he could affect a passable French Swiss accent while speaking French. During his prewar visits to Switzerland people had noted a Swiss inflection in his speech, which he had purposely worked to adopt. Even with a perfect French Swiss accent, though, his plan was a long shot. The British were suspicious of all those who claimed to be Swiss and routinely held them until they could confirm their identity. If Killinger's letter to his sister reached her, and if she contacted Pastor Epars, and if he agreed to go along with the plan, it just might work. But there were a lot of "ifs" in the equation.

The next requirement was to create a history that explained why his seaman's papers showed no employment for several years. The papers contained detailed entries about every ship a seaman had served on, including the name of the captain, the route, and the cargo. All that information had to be accurate, or the British would spot the forgery. The papers Killinger had bought on the waterfront proved to be useful despite the age and physical differences between himself and the former owner. Using the papers as a guide, the forger created a seafaring history for Jean Epars from 1906 to 1912. To fill a blank space from 1912 to 1916 he would claim to have been working in Bogotá, Colombia, as a driver and auto mechanic who had been drawn to North America, specifically New York, by the high wartime wages being offered to seamen. He had made the trip from Barranquilla, Colombia, as a steerage passenger. Whether or not the British bought the story would depend on Killinger's skill as a liar.

Armed with his counterfeit papers and identity, Killinger looked for work among the seediest job brokers on the waterfront. Finding a job was not easy. There were many ships bound for England and France that needed crewmen but very few bound for Norway. And those few had full crews. He briefly considered bribing a sailor to let him take his place in the crew but dismissed the plan when he realized that he would also have to create an entirely new set of papers in the man's name.

He finally landed a berth on the Holland-America Line's SS *Noordam* as a fireman. The *Noordam* was one of the few ships that still operated regularly between New York and Europe, and she frequently carried German intelligence agents, spies, and saboteurs back and forth across the Atlantic. The British were aware of that and made a special effort to examine those ships when they made the required stop at Ramsgate. In August 1915 the British had captured the spy and saboteur Kapitänleutnant Franz von Rintelen, known as the "Dark Invader," who was returning to Germany on the *Noordam* on a forged Swiss passport under the name Emile V. Gasché.

When Killinger reported on the *Noordam* as Jean Epars, the captain examined his papers, asked about the blank period after 1912, and appeared to accept the explanation. The most hazardous part of the trip was yet to come, however. There was the overriding threat that the British would see through his counterfeit papers. Killinger was then just a few weeks away from his twenty-third birthday, but his seaman's papers described a man who had to be at least six years older based on his work history. There was also the danger that a fellow crewman would discover who he really was and turn him in for the reward. Further, despite his naval training, he was not qualified or experienced enough to pass as a fireman on a commercial vessel. He might have passed himself off as a deck hand, but even that is doubtful. What saved him was the unexpected arrival of several British passengers the following morning.

He was working on a cargo hold ventilator when a large group of men and women came on board accompanied by news cameramen and reporters. Passengers were one thing, but Killinger had had his fill of the press. The cause of the excitement and the reason for the reporters' presence soon became evident. The passengers had been on the SS *Appam* when the German raider SMS *Möwe* took her as a war prize on 16 January 1916 off the Canary Islands. In addition to a valuable cargo of palm oil, the *Appam* was carrying 160 civilian passengers, among them 20 German nationals. Eight of the Germans were POWs, and nine were German reservists whom the British were taking to England. There were also three German women. Among the British personnel on the *Appam* were the British governor of Sierra Leon and Nigeria and four officers and twenty seamen of the Royal Navy.

While she was still outside the three-mile limit the *Möwe* took on board the German POWs, the reservists, and the three women, as well as the officers and men of the Royal Navy. Because the *Möwe* was headed home, her captain, Korvettenkapitän Nikolaus Burggraf und Graf zu Dohna-Schlodien, transferred all his civilian prisoners to the *Appam* and sent her into Newport News, Virginia, under the command of Leutnant zur See Hans Berg and twenty-one German sailors. The Germans released the passengers in Newport News, and many of them went directly to New York to book passage to Britain. The United States promptly interned Leutnant zur See Berg and his prize crew.

The arrival of the *Appam* passengers was big news in the United States, and the press hounded them, following them to New York and then to the *Noordam*. Killinger was working on a ventilator that was very close to the former *Appam* passengers when a reporter asked him in English, "Are you from the *Appam*?" Killinger pretended not to understand, and the reporter went away. But the incident scared him, and he immediately put down his tools and walked off the ship.

He figured that having jumped ship before the *Noordam* sailed would blacklist him on the New York waterfront and decided to go to Baltimore to make a fresh start. He still had the addresses and names of captains whom he could contact for passage that Reicke had given him. He took the train to Baltimore that day, arriving there on the evening of 6 February

1916. Killinger had by this time become an expert at finding the sleaziest accommodations available and fitting in with the local crowd. The hotel he chose fit the bill exactly, and the inhabitants were the type who asked no questions. He later described the hotel as "rundown and seedy. The ground floor bar attracted all sorts of waterfront life including several blacks. You could buy almost anything in the bar. It was a hangout for prostitutes, thieves, and seamen who had hit rock bottom. The upper floor rooms were rented by the hour. It was for my purposes the perfect place to stay."[9]

Having obtained a room, his next stop was a secondhand shop where he bought clothing that he thought was typical of what a merchant seaman would wear on land, hoping to make himself appear more believable to the local waterfront characters and later to the British authorities. He had a photo taken of himself in his "new" clothes that he included with his counterfeit seaman's papers. The effect was a cross between an Apache dancer and a railroad hobo.

The following evening he walked into a waterfront bar and ordered a beer. He was working on his second beer when a man joined him and they struck up a conversation. The newcomer was a Norwegian seaman whose ship, the SS *Storfjeld*, was scheduled to sail the next morning at 8 a.m. Quick to see the opportunity, Killinger suggested they find a table and do some serious drinking. Killinger plied his new friend with whisky until the Norwegian passed out facedown on the table. Killinger figured that the seaman was out for the night and might not be well enough in the morning to make the sailing. He was right.

Killinger was at the hiring office when it opened at 6 a.m., and so was the *Storfjeld*'s captain. Killinger could not be sure it was the *Storfjeld*'s, captain, but he figured that the odds were pretty good. He deferentially allowed the captain to enter first. The officer went straight to the clerk and told him that he needed an able seaman to replace one who had gone missing. The hiring agent told the captain that able seamen were hard to find, and those willing to go to a port anywhere in Europe were even rarer because few were willing to run the gauntlet of U-boats and mines.

Killinger stood back, feigning indifference to what was being said, but made his move as soon as the captain gave the clerk the ship's name— *Storfjeld*. He walked to the window and told the clerk that he was an able seaman looking for a berth. The captain stepped in and asked Killinger to sign on with his ship.

"Where are you going?" Killinger asked.

"Norway."

"No thanks; too dangerous. I prefer South America."

"I'll pay you twenty dollars a month," the captain said.

Killinger snorted. "That's not enough. I can get twenty going to Rio and back."

"I'll give you thirty-five dollars to Norway," the captain said, upping the ante.

"Make that a round trip, thirty-five each way." Killinger thought the British would be less likely to question his papers if he was signed on for a round trip. The captain agreed to thirty-five each way, and the deal was done.[10]

The employment clerk quickly prepared the papers certifying Killinger as an able seaman signed as a deck hand on the SS *Storfjeld* for the voyage to Skien, Norway, and return. Killinger signed them and left with the captain. So far, things were falling into place, but there was still a chance that the missing seaman would show up at the ship.

When they arrived at the *Storfjeld* the captain told Killinger to join a work crew carrying sacks of corn onto the ship. There were several hundred sacks to be lugged up the gangplank and stacked in the hold. Killinger, who was not in shape for this sort of heavy labor, felt his legs tremble as he huffed and puffed up and down the gangplank. He gritted his teeth and "worked like an animal, knowing that the sooner we finished the sooner we would go to sea. My only worry was that my drunken friend would regain his senses and arrive before we put to sea."

The seaman was still missing when the men finished loading the corn shortly after 9 a.m. Killinger worked with the foredeck line handlers casting off the *Storfjeld* as a tug pulled her away from the wharf. The after-lines came in, the tug shifted to the port side, and the freighter moved into the main channel. Killinger breathed a sigh of relief. In a short time the ship was headed down the Patapsco River for Chesapeake Bay and the Atlantic. As he watched the shoreline slide past, Killinger thought to himself, "Everything has worked up to now; all that I need is to go unnoticed by the British."

TRANSATLANTIC

10 February–6 March 1916

uilt in 1899, the *Storfjeld* was a typical eight-knot, three-island tramp, so called because her maximum speed was eight knots and along her length she had three raised sections—islands—that rose above the main deck: her forepeak, midship superstructure, and quarterdeck. The name "tramp" did not mean she was a rust bucket. It meant that she would carry general cargo to any port in the world without regard to a regular schedule, destination, or route. Three-island tramps were the workhorses and backbone of the world's merchant fleet before the advent of the container ship.

The *Storfjeld* passed through the Virginia Capes and entered the Atlantic on 10 February 1916. She could cross the Atlantic from Baltimore to Skien, Norway, in twenty-four days, but the actual time at sea varied from one voyage to the next. In bad weather the trip could take a full month. Since she was going to Norway, her captain would take the ship around Scotland, across the North Sea, and through the Skagerrak. There would be an unscheduled stop included in the leg around Scotland at Stornoway.

Since Sir Edward Hawke's victory over the French in the Battle of Quiberon Bay in November 1759, the Royal Navy had been using the strategy of continuous blockade in time of war. During World War I the British blockade was virtually airtight. Any seaborne traffic attempting to reach a northern European port had to either pass through the western approaches and into the English Channel or go north around Scotland and pass between Scotland and the Orkneys to enter the North Sea. The Royal Navy maintained powerful standing patrols across both routes. Until nearly the end of the war, German U-boats could go from the North Sea to the Atlantic and back through either the English Channel and Dover Strait or north around Scotland, though after 1916 the High Seas Fleet boats used the northern route exclusively. But there was really no way for surface vessels to slip through the blockade at any point. Any surface vessel coming from the Atlantic to Germany or anywhere else in the North Sea was going to be stopped and examined by Royal Navy personnel. The Royal Navy claimed this right under the prize rules as defined in the 1909 London Convention. A series of subsequent orders in council had expanded the contraband lists and tightened the blockade.

Under the prize rules a belligerent power's warship could stop and board any neutral vessel at sea. If the neutral ship appeared to be carrying contraband to an enemy power, the ship was seized, and the prize rules demanded that the ship be taken into port for examination if possible. If that was not possible, the belligerent's warship could sink the vessel, but only after seeing to the safety of the ship's crew and passengers. It was a clumsy and difficult-to-enforce rule, but the Royal Navy had the ships and the will to make it work. Vessels bound for any European port were taken into one of several British harbors where examiners waited to go over the ship's manifest and cargo and interrogate her crew and passengers. If the Royal Navy examiners found anything suspicious about the ship, crew, or passengers, they detained the ship and all on board.

By February 1916 the Royal Navy had perfected the search and examination of ships to a precise procedure. An armed boarding party took the ship into the nearest British port for examination, where another boarding party, composed of specialists, came on board and separated to carry out their assignments. Some went belowdecks and thoroughly searched the ship for stowaways and hidden contraband. They overlooked nothing, even unbolting inspection plates and crawling into virtually inaccessible hiding places. Another group examined the ship's papers, including the manifests and bills of lading, while another group examined the cargo itself. The companies named in the papers were compared with a list of company names on the "black list." Any cargo consigned to a blacklisted company was seized. Another, much smaller group examined the passengers individually with the same thoroughness. Any passenger who seemed in any way suspicious was detained.

Killinger had about three weeks to work out a plan for getting past the British examiners.[1] In the meantime, he was a "deck ape" trying to avoid making a mistake that would reveal that he was not a professional seaman or a French Swiss national. Though the *Storfjeld* was a Norwegian-flagged vessel and her crew was international, the common language among them was English. His cover identity as a French-Swiss national made his slight German accent when speaking English a liability.

Before he boarded the *Noordam* in New York he had taken a risky step to make his appearance more seaman-like that could have caused serious health problems. Concerned that his relatively soft hands would give him away to the other crewmembers, and later to the British inspectors, he decided that he needed reddened, scarred worker's hands. To achieve that look he nicked his fingers in several places with a sharp knife and then soaked his hands in fuel that had been used to clean rusted metal. His fingers swelled and "the rust particles stuck in the cuts," and a few days later he had the "proper seaman's fists" he wanted and was confident that the "deception would not be easily recognized." His seaman's hands had probably helped to convince the *Storfjeld*'s captain that he was an experienced deck hand.

But appearances alone would not hide the fact that he was something other than an old salt. He had to act the part too, and that meant going about his daily tasks with an air of confidence and efficiency. He had picked up the basics as a midshipman during his training cruise on SMS *Vineta* and his time on SMS *Berlin*. He could swab decks and chip paint with the best of them. But there was more to being a deck hand than that, and much of it was hard labor. "In my entire life," Killinger later wrote, "I never worked as hard as I did during those four weeks."

The *Storfjeld* carried three able seamen and three seamen on her muster roll as deck hands. Their duties were general maintenance and repair, including chipping paint and repainting, bilge cleaning, splicing steel cable, and other general labor. In addition, the three able seamen stood watches as the ship's helmsmen, each man standing two four-hour watches. He fumbled occasionally—splicing steel cable, for example, was not something he did well—but he managed not to attract any negative attention.

Killinger had learned a valuable lesson from his experience with J. Fred Havey, and while he was still in New York he had gotten the names of two freighters and had memorized their routes and the ports they visited. He went to a library and looked up the ports in an encyclopedia so that when asked where he had previously sailed he could give a believable answer. He had more than one occasion to use his book-acquired knowledge, and he kept his answers short. As much as possible he played the role of a man of few words and something of a loner. But there was one exception.

One of the seamen was an illiterate Finn who had been at sea for many years. Other than his own language he spoke only a smattering of English, Russian, and German. The Finn was friendly, helpful, and not too bright, which made him the ideal crewmember to befriend. There was no way the man would see through Killinger to uncover his real identity and purpose. The Finn made the transatlantic trip regularly and had gone through the British examination every time. Though the language barrier made conversation with him difficult, Killinger frequently grilled him about what to expect. He asked only the Finn about the upcoming examination because he was sure that too many questions would arouse suspicion among the other deck crewmen, and the British paid a three-pound reward to any crewman who disclosed a German among them. He was taking a chance with the Finn, but he believed that the man was too simple-minded to be a real threat. The Finn's answers to his questions about the examination were most discouraging; Killinger concluded that his chances of slipping past the examiners were very slight.

Most important, perhaps, was how to explain to the British examiners why a Swiss citizen of French extraction spoke with a German accent. He also had to be doubly sure that he always responded in English to anything that was said to him in German, a common trick the British examiners used on those they suspected of being German. Killinger was determined not to fall for that.

The fact that he was trying to pass himself off as French Swiss made it almost a dead certainty that the British would detain him; in addition, he was new to the ship and the British had no record of having examined him previously on another ship. No matter how much he pondered the obstacles, he could not find a way around them. As the ship neared the British patrol lines, his morale sank. And then he found a reason to hope.

During one of his laborious conversations with the Finn he learned that on a previous voyage the captain had signed on a former crewman from the German auxiliary cruiser SS *Kronprinz Wilhelm*, which was interned in Norfolk, Virginia, on 11 April 1915. The captain signed the German on as an engineer, knowing full well who and what he was. When the British said they were going to detain the man for further questioning, the captain had vouched for him, telling the authorities that the man was vital to the ship's operation and the *Storfjeld* would be unable to continue her voyage if they detained him. If the Finn's story was true, Killinger might have a chance. There certainly was precedent.

Immediately after the war started, hundreds of German military reservists who were living in the United States tried to return to Germany, and many of the early birds made it before the British had the blockade firmly in place. Beginning in September 1914, some of the German crewmen, usually officers, from the German ships that were interned in U.S. ports also tried to get back to Germany because they held reserve commissions in the Imperial German Navy. The British became steadily more efficient in screening people, however, and by November 1914 the door was effectively closed. But a few did continue to slip through until the early part of 1915, and German saboteurs were still passing through the blockade en route to the United States as late as October 1916. So an engineer from the SS *Kronprinz Wilhelm* might have made it past the examiners in the spring of 1915 if he was very lucky.

Killinger's situation was considerably different from that of the *Kronprinz Wilhelm*'s engineer because the captain could easily manage without him for the short remainder of the trip. Further, if the British detained Killinger, the captain could pocket his pay. The captain had to have an incentive to help him. Killinger naively thought that if he told the captain who and what he really was, the captain would vouch for him as he had for the engineer.

The following evening he paid a visit to the captain's cabin. Without any small talk or buildup, he simply stated, "Captain, I am a German." He might have done better had he led up to that announcement with more information about his circumstances.

The captain shrugged and said, "Then the British will arrest you."

The absolute finality of the captain's reply stunned Killinger; this was not the cooperation he had expected. His momentary surprise quickly turned to anger. His approach became threatening and aggressive. He told the captain that he knew about the German engineer whom the captain had vouched for and threatened to tell the British about it if they detained him. The captain's response was another shrug with, "Go ahead and tell them. I'll just deny it."

"They might believe you, but there are witnesses on board," Killinger countered.

The captain remained unimpressed. "So the story is true," he said dismissively with another shrug. "But I knew nothing about him being a German until I was in Norway."

Killinger recognized that he was up against a hard case who held the high cards and knew it. "I can tell them that he paid you a large bribe in Baltimore to sign on as an engineer, with a promise of an additional bribe when you landed him in Norway." Killinger was shooting in the dark on that one, but he hit the target right on the mark. He added, "On that the British will arrest you, your ship will be seized, and your company will be placed on the blacklist."

For a moment, it looked as though the captain was going to do something violent, but that moment passed as the captain came to the realization that Killinger too might hold some high cards. What Killinger had said about the British seizing the ship was exactly right. And that was something the captain very much wanted to avoid. The captain certainly had a problem on his hands, but it was a manageable problem, and he grudgingly agreed to do his best.

Killinger refused to be put off with assurances. He wanted all the help the captain could provide, and he made that clear when he told the captain, "You do your best. But if they detain me, I will tell them about the previous German."

When Killinger left the captain's cabin, he was anything but satisfied. He strongly doubted that the captain would act on his behalf, and even if the captain *did* want to help Killinger there was little he could do. The best course for the captain was simply to sit back and let the British take Killinger, knowing that he would carry out his threat to talk about the earlier German. The captain was on reasonably solid ground if he steadfastly denied any previous knowledge about Killinger's true identity and held to the story that he was unaware of any German having been in his crew previously. The captain still held the high cards.

On 29 February 1916 a British auxiliary cruiser stopped the *Storfjeld* under the prize regulations and came alongside close enough for a six-man boarding party to cross to the *Storfjeld*. The Royal Navy ensign in charge of the boarding party told the *Storfjeld*'s captain to follow the cruiser toward Stornoway on the Isle of Lewis in the Outer Hebrides. Five hours later a patrol boat replaced the cruiser and took the lead for another five hours. The handoffs continued until a British light cruiser met them just off Stornoway and led the *Storfjeld* to the harbor entrance, where the inspection crew came on board from a smaller craft.

The boarding party's purpose was to make the initial examination of the ship's papers and cargo, and to search the ship for stowaways. They also searched the crew's quarters for anything that the shore examiners could use in their interrogations. When the searches and examinations were completed, the harbor pilot came on board and the *Storfjeld* was taken to a special berth reserved for inspections and placed under heavy guard.

Killinger now entered the third, and most dangerous, phase of his escape. In most cases, the third escape phase occurs when an escapee crosses a frontier between enemy territory and neutral territory. In this case, however, even if he made it through the British inspection, he would not arrive in neutral territory until the ship docked in Skien. Stornoway was Killinger's moment of truth.

As soon as the ship was made fast in the berth, two Royal Navy officers and a guard assembled the entire crew outside the captain's cabin. Every crewman had his papers in his hand ready to hand them over to the British inspectors. The crew examination was straightforward and thorough. A guard was posted at the cabin door and an officer called crewmen into the cabin one at a time. After each crewman went through the door, the guard closed it behind him.

Inside the cabin, the Royal Navy inspectors, with the *Storfjeld*'s captain watching, examined the crewman's papers, comparing what was written with what they could observe. Then they questioned the man about the information in the papers, particularly about any gaps in it. If the man had previously been through an examination and his papers bore a Royal Navy inspector's stamp, the examination was very brief and at its end an inspector told the sailor to wait outside. When the crewman emerged from the room the guard directed him to stand in a spot away from the unexamined crewmen. If the man being questioned could *not* satisfy the inspectors, he was taken through another door and detained ashore.

Killinger could do nothing but stand quietly while waiting for his turn in the captain's cabin. He knew without doubt that he would not make it through the examination because his papers identified him as Swiss, which was a sure ticket to the detention lockup. It was impossible at this point to slip away and hide on the ship, if such an option had ever existed. He also accepted the reality that, given the way the British were handling the inspections, the captain could do nothing for him even if he wanted to. His clever plan was suddenly out the window, and he was presented with a situation for which he had not prepared. If he was going to do something to save himself, he had to do it soon.

He carefully studied the crewmen around him, looking for something that might help him. As he did, he started to worry that one of them might expose him. It would take only a nod and a pointed finger to get him arrested and earn the crewman a three-pound reward. He did not know any of them very well, but he hoped they were anti-British, and therefore not willing to help them just for the reward. He calmed down when he realized that the possibility of a crewman betraying him was irrelevant; he was as good as caught anyway.

The inspectors had examined about half the crew when an opportunity suddenly presented itself. There were now two separate groups standing on the deck outside the captain's door. One group was waiting to be examined; the other was composed of men who had been through the examination. The distance separating the two groups was about ten or twelve feet. The only thing that kept the groups separated and in place was the armed guard standing at the door. Some commotion on the dock caused the guard to leave his post and step around the corner. He was away for only a moment, but in that moment Killinger quickly stepped from one group to the other.

It was an amazing piece of good luck, made more amazing by the fact that none of the crew raised an alarm. None of the men standing outside the door could have missed seeing him make the move, and every one of them either knew or suspected why he did it. Speaking up would have earned a man the easiest three pounds he ever got, but no one said a word. Luck aside, the move showed that Killinger was quick to see an opening and bold enough to take the opportunity. On the other hand, he had nothing to lose.

Three days after the British had brought the *Storfjeld* into Stornoway they released her. The passage across the North Sea and through the Skagerrak went without incident, and on the morning of 4 March 1916 the *Storfjeld* put into Skien. Killinger immediately left the ship, took the train to Oslo (then called Kristiania), and found a room for the night. He sent a telegram to his family saying that he was safe and would be back in Germany shortly, and then took a hot bath—his first in more than a month.

He reported to the German embassy the following morning in high spirits, but he did not get the reception he expected. He had spent three months making people believe he was not a German, and now he had to reverse the role and make them believe he was a German. Lacking any identity papers that would have established his true identity, he was unable to convince the embassy official that he was a German naval officer who had escaped from Siberia.

When Killinger described how he and three others had jumped from a train in Manchuria in the dead of winter and had walked across China, the official said that that was impossible. Killinger's claim that he had just slipped through the British blockade without proper papers was even more impossible. His shabby appearance did nothing to help his case. The official asked why, if he was really a German naval officer, he was not properly dressed in uniform instead of looking like a bum.

Killinger continued to plead his case, but the official would not budge. He was up against the German bureaucratic mind at its worst. It was beyond the civilian official's grasp that a German officer would be shabbily dressed and without proper identification. And the story about the escape from Siberia and getting through the blockade had to be pure fantasy. Finally Killinger made a chip in the stone wall. He managed to get the official to provide him with a temporary pass that described him as an "alleged German naval officer who had allegedly escaped from Siberia and is en route Germany." The official added the notation that the information was based on Killinger's claim, for which there was no corroboration, and reluctantly gave him fifty kronen.

That afternoon, 5 March 1916, Killinger took the overnight train to Halsingbord, Sweden, where he would catch the ferry to Helsingør, Denmark. He had just taken a seat in the third-class car when a man came up to him and said he was a police detective and demanded his papers. Killinger snapped. He had been on the run for eleven months, had lived under the threat of exposure every day, and had squeaked through the British blockade by the sheerest serendipity. He was now twenty-four hours from his goal, in a neutral country, and this man was threatening him. He leaned toward the man and told him in English, "Go to hell!" He added that unless the man could prove he had the authority to question him, he would call the conductor and have him detained.

He knew that he was taking an enormous risk by challenging the man. If in fact he *was* a Norwegian police officer, he would certainly arrest him on the spot. But it became clear that the man was not a detective when he was unable to produce any identification, and Killinger concluded that he must be a British agent. If that were the case, the man might have seen Killinger enter and leave the German embassy and followed him to the train. Since the train was headed south, he probably assumed that Killinger was headed for Germany. And in 1916, any military-age male leaving the German embassy and taking a train toward Germany had to be a reservist going home to join the army.

On the other hand, the man might have been nothing more than a petty crook who saw an opportunity to prey on someone who looked like a bum. For the most part, the Germans' paranoia about British agents and spies being everywhere was just that—unwarranted paranoia. Even if the stranger had been a British agent, he had no authority to arrest anyone, not even a German soldier or reservist. And the Swedish authorities were unlikely to accept the prisoner anyway because Sweden was pro-Germany during World War I.

In any event, Killinger had successfully called the man's bluff. Faced with determined opposition, the man hurried away, and Killinger did not see him again. The remainder of the overnight trip was uneventful, but he did not sleep. Worry about having been accosted by a possible British agent and excitement about being back in Germany the next day kept him wide awake.

The train arrived in Halsingbord at dawn, and Killinger went directly to the ferry landing and boarded the ferry that took him across the sound to Helsingør, Denmark. At midmorning he boarded a train for Copenhagen, where he changed trains for the ferry landing at Gjedser, arriving there at 2 p.m. on 6 March—eleven months to the day after he had been captured. From there he took the ferry to Warnemünde and entered Germany that evening.

There was no hero's welcome waiting for him when he set foot on German soil. The German embassy in Copenhagen had sent a telegram to the police in Warnemünde to be on the alert for a man trying to enter Germany claiming to be an escaped German naval officer. The telegram included Killinger's physical description. Indeed, the man who had accosted him on the train might have been a German embassy official who was trying to uncover Killinger's real identity. Obviously, someone in the embassy suspected he was a spy for someone.

The Landsturm guards who were posted at the Warnemünde ferry landing had no trouble spotting him because he jumped from the ferry onto the landing even before the ferry had been made fast to the dock. Two burly guards moved in, grabbed him by the arms, and roughly hustled him to a police inspector. Hurriedly, Killinger spilled out his tale of having escaped from a train in Siberia and identified himself as Fähnrich zur See Erich Killinger. Nodding his head, the police inspector said in a noncommittal, flat tone, "Yes, I know. You have already been reported."

Killinger demanded to be taken to the commanding officer of the border police detachment, but the police inspector made it clear that he was in no position to make demands. He asked Killinger for identification, and Killinger handed him the pass that the embassy official in Oslo had given him. The police inspector looked at the pass, smiled derisively, and said, "No German official would be dumb enough to write something like this." Apparently, the police inspector had never been to the German embassy in Oslo.

The naval seaplane station at Warnemünde was only a mile or two away, and Killinger asked the police inspector to call there and ask if anyone recognized his name. The police inspector agreed and had the guards bring Killinger to the police office a few yards away while he made the call. The phone call was a long shot for Killinger, but perhaps someone there would recall his name; after all, there had not been very many naval aviators in the autumn of 1914 and spring of 1915. The police inspector completed his call and told Killinger that someone from the air station was coming to look at him. He obviously still had doubts.

An hour later a naval officer arrived at the office; when he stepped through the door, Killinger knew that he was saved. The officer was Clifford von Tempsky, who had been with him and von Gorrissen on the *Friedrich Carl* in October 1914 and had gone north to Memel with them on the *Glyndwr* in 1915. His first words when he saw Killinger were, "Erich! You're alive!"

GERMANY

6 March 1916–9 March 1920

There was no fanfare or hero's welcome for Erich Killinger after his return to Germany. The General Staff did not promote him, decorate him, or make him a national icon as they had with Gunther Plüschow in July 1915. Plüschow made a big splash because he was the first man to make it back to Germany from a POW camp in England. The only public recognition Killinger received was through the publication of his book, *Die Abenteuer des Ostseefliegers*, as part of the Ullstein War Books series in 1917 and a photo spread in the 18 March 1917 issue of the Ullstein-owned newspaper, *Berliner Illustrirte Zeitung*.[1] Why was he largely ignored after his epic journey?

Being the first escaped POW to make it through the blockade was certainly an accomplishment worthy of high praise and recognition. But the propaganda value of that accomplishment was somewhat diminished by the fact that several hundred reservists had also made it through the blockade, though at an earlier time and under less difficult conditions.

Looks might have been another factor. Plüschow was movie star handsome and fit the image of the daring German aviator. Killinger was tall and reedy, almost stork-like, and when he arrived back in Germany he was still a back-seater rather than a pilot.

The other, and probably more important reason for the lack of publicity was security. Plüschow had escaped from Donington Hall and made it back to Germany without any help from the Foreign Office–run escape pipeline, not because he was more resourceful than Killinger but because the pipeline did not operate in England. So the Germans had nothing to keep secret about Plüschow's escape. He was the perfect propaganda poster boy.

Once Killinger and his three friends made it to Mukden, though, they had entered the German pipeline for escapees—a system the Germans did not want publicized. German newspapers reported only that he had escaped from Russian captivity in Siberia, had returned to Germany safely, and was now back in the war. So Plüschow got the publicity, and Killinger went back to the war.

But Killinger was not entirely ignored. The Imperial German Navy had already promoted him to Leutnant zur See on 18 February 1916, eleven days before the Royal Navy stopped the *Storfjeld* and took her into Stornoway. That was five months *after* his classmates in Crew 13 had been routinely promoted as a group, but he had not been overlooked at that time. His promotion had gone through with the others, but because the Navy did not know if he was dead or alive, Killinger's promotion was put on hold pending confirmation of his status. Now that he was home, his promotion became effective and was backdated to 18 February 1916, and the single stripe of a Leutnant zur See adorned his coat sleeves.

The day after arriving in Germany he went to Berlin, where he was directed to write a detailed report of his experiences. He spent seven days writing four detailed narratives covering the time from his takeoff on 6 April 1915 until his arrival in Germany on 6 March 1916. Killinger was the first escapee to make it back to Germany using the transpacific-USA-Atlantic route, and this was the first extensive account of the route the Germans had received. But the most important information the Germans got from Killinger's lengthy report was an inside look at the efficiency of the British blockade.

Killinger remained in Berlin being wined and dined, seeing the sights, and giving high-ranking naval officers a firsthand account of his escape experience until he received orders on 17 March to report to the seaplane station at Zeebrugge (Seeflugstation I) after completing pilot training at Warnemünde.

On 16 March the commanding officer at Seeflugstation I, Oberleutnant zur See Bernhard von Tschirschky, had received a memorandum from the Naval Staff in Berlin suggesting that he recommend Killinger for the Iron Cross, First Class, apparently on the basis of his escape from the Russians. On 28 March 1916 von Tschirschky replied that he would not make the recommendation, saying that Killinger already had the Iron Cross, Second

Class, and since he was to be stationed in Flanders he would have ample opportunities to distinguish himself and earn the recommendation.[2]

One might assume that when an admiral in Berlin "suggested" to a lieutenant in Flanders that he make a recommendation, the lieutenant would hop to it. But in the larger scheme of things, Bernhard von Tschirschky was no mere minion. His full name was Bernhard Friedrich Wilhelm Leonard Richard Otto von Tschirschky und Bögendorff, and his family lineage, going back to 1329, included big names in both the Sachsen and imperial governments. So given his lineage and his yard-long name, maybe the Admiralty Staff gave him some leeway. Or he may have refused to make the recommendation because *he* had not yet received the Iron Cross, First Class, and because Killinger was something of a celebrity hero while he was not. On the other hand, maybe von Tschirschky was one of those officers who felt strongly that medals should not be awarded simply for doing one's duty. It was a prisoner's duty to escape, or at least to try, and perhaps he believed that Killinger did not deserve to be rewarded for having done what he was expected to do. In any case, the Naval Staff seems not to have punished von Tschirschky when he did not act on the "suggestion"—quite the opposite, in fact.

Among the several awards Killinger did receive was the Order of the Zähringen Lion, Third Class, with Swords. The medal was not in the same class as the Iron Cross, First Class, but was much more impressive looking than the rather plain Iron Cross. He also received the Lübeck Hanseatic Cross and the Hamburg Hanseatic Cross. Each of the three Hanseatic city-states—Bremen, Hamburg, and Lübeck—issued its own cross for military merit, and Killinger was one of the relatively few people to receive two of the crosses. Another two-cross recipient was Rittmeister Manfred Albrecht Freiherr von Richthofen, the Red Baron.

On 19 September 1916, one day after receiving his pilot's badge in Warnemünde, Killinger reported to his new assignment at Zeebrugge. On arrival he learned that von Tschirschky had been promoted to Kapitän-leutnant on 1 September and had gone to Sylt to command the seaplane station there. Oberleutnant zur See Friedrich Christiansen was the new commanding officer of Seeflugstation I.

At that time Seeflugstation I was equipped with four types of float-planes: the Friedrichshafen FF.33e, a two-seat reconnaissance aircraft that had been in service since 1915 and could carry a small bomb load; the single-seat Albatros W.4, a fighter that had been in service since June 1916; seven Hansa-Brandenburg KDW single-seat fighters; and seven Friedrichshafen FF.33f single-seat fighters, a variant of the 33e that had been in service since June 1916.[3] In May 1917 a fourth type of fighter would arrive, the Rumpler 6B1, a single-seater specifically designed for coastal defense.

As the war dragged on, Seeflugstation I received Hansa-Brandenburg W.12 and Hansa-Brandenburg W.19 aircraft, which combined the role of fighter, reconnaissance, and bomber. Both were two-seaters that featured Ernst Heinkel's unique inverted tail design with the vertical stabilizer and rudder pointing downward below the fuselage. The design gave the observer-gunner a clear field of fire in a half-hemisphere above and behind the aircraft. The Hansa-Brandenburg W.29 single-seat fighter, also designed by Heinkel, entered service in the summer of 1918. It was a low-wing monoplane that was strongly built and very maneuverable.

Seeflugstation I was located on the Zeebrugge Mole, an enormous seawall that was one of "the most colossal constructions of its kind in the world."[4] Before the war, Zeebrugge harbor had functioned as a commercial port that handled mainly ferries from Britain, for which there were two large goods sheds and a passenger terminal near the west end of the mole. When the Germans occupied Zeebrugge, they built the air station where the passenger terminal was, using that building for headquarters and the goods sheds for stores. They also built four hangars against the mole wall and smaller buildings for fuel and ammunition. Also associated with the passenger terminal were two large cargo cranes that the Germans used to set the seaplanes on the water and to hoist them back onto the mole floor.

From the point where it left the shore at its western end to the lighthouse on its eastern end the mole was about 1.5 miles long. Inside the curved breakwater was a three-hundred-acre harbor that was ideal for seaplane operations. The eighty-yard-wide mole floor provided ample room for the seaplane base, and the two-track railroad that came out to the old passenger terminal made it possible to send airplanes to shops and repair halls at Marinekorps Flugplatz Lissewege a half mile away for major repairs.[5]

Seeflugstation I was assigned to patrol the Hoofden, an area encompassing the southern part of the North Sea and defined roughly by a line drawn along latitude 52° N from Scheveningen in the Netherlands to Yarmouth on the British east coast, then down the east coast of Britain to a line drawn at about 51.5° N from the mouth of the Thames to

Ostend in Belgium, and from there north along a line from Ostend back to Scheveningen.

Aircraft from the station conducted reconnaissance missions, bombed targets on the British east coast, attacked units of the British Auxiliary Patrol, and provided air defense at Zeebrugge and Ostend. Except for air defense, most of the missions used the two-seat aircraft, some of which were equipped with radios and could carry bombs. In addition to air defense and escorting the bombers, the single-seat fighters also attacked targets of opportunity, as in the case of the attack on the British submarine *C-25* on 6 July 1918.

When Killinger arrived on 19 September, Kapitänleutnant Friedrich Christiansen appointed him his adjutant, but the staff assignment did not prevent him from flying, and it soon became evident that von Tschirschky had been right when he predicted that Killinger would have ample opportunity to distinguish himself. In fact, Killinger's Zeebrugge assignment apparently got him all the action he had craved as a newly minted airman, and he was awarded the Iron Cross, First Class, on 1 October 1916.[6] Killinger never became an ace, which required shooting down five enemy aircraft, and his name is not listed in the published works that list World War I aerial victories, but on 25 January 1918 the state of Baden awarded him the prestigious Knight's Cross of the Military Karl Friedrich Merit-Order. Of the 288 that were awarded during World War I, only 8 of the medals went to aviators, and Killinger was the sole naval aviator to receive one.

Seeflugstation I provided protection for two types of U-boats that operated under Marinekorps command: coastal boats that were identified by the letters UB and the boat's number, and small minelayers that were identified by the letters UC followed by the boat's number. A total of 231 UB and UC boats were built during the war, and 45 percent of them were based in Flanders as part of the Marinekorps. The other 55 percent were distributed through three commands: the High Seas Fleet based at Emden and Wilhelmshaven, the Mediterranean based at Pola, and the U-boat school.[7]

The Marinekorps had two missions: to anchor the German army's right flank and to protect the U-boats that were a major part of its force. As a fighter pilot stationed on the Flanders coast, Killinger probably spent a lot of time defending against British bombers that were en route to bomb the Bruges U-boat base and the U-boat facilities at Zeebrugge and Ostend.

The U-boats under the Marinekorps' command were based in Bruges, where the command headquarters, air-raid-proof U-boat bunkers, and repair shops were located. They entered the North Sea through two canals: the eight-mile-long Zeebrugge-Bruges canal and the eleven-mile-long Ostend-Bruges canal. The British had been making plans since 1916 to close both Zeebrugge and Ostend in order to "cork the bottle" and seal in the U-boats at Bruges. And on the night of 22–23 April 1918, the British took the war to Killinger and all the airmen, gunners, and naval infantrymen at Zeebrugge for just that purpose.[8]

The British launched simultaneous raids on Zeebrugge and Ostend—a huge undertaking—with the intent to block both Zeebrugge and Ostend harbors by sinking cement-laden block ships in the canal entrances. The raid at Ostend was a complete failure because the two block ships, HMS *Sirius* and HMS *Brilliant*, ran aground outside the harbor entrance.[9] The assault on Zeebrugge, a wild and bloody affair that involved three block ships, three troop ships, and a submarine laden with high explosives, was at least a partial success.

The battle opened at 11:50 p.m. on 22 April when the German defenders on the mole spotted the approaching British attack force and opened fire. The British plan called for an infantry landing on the mole to disrupt the defenses and distract the Germans' attention from the three block ships that would enter the harbor after the landing got under way. A third element of the attack was a C-class submarine loaded with explosives that was to ram itself under the railroad viaduct and explode, blowing a gap in the viaduct that would prevent German reinforcements from reaching the mole.

Under heavy, accurate fire from the defenders, the three troop ships—HMS *Vindictive* and two civilian ferries, the *Daffodil* and *Iris*—turned to lay alongside the mole wall. The *Iris* and *Daffodil* were unable to land their troops, and the *Vindictive* came alongside the mole 340 yards beyond her intended position; the surge caused by her speed and draft kept her from making fast. The *Daffodil* was diverted to act as a tug and press the old cruiser against the wall.

The explosives submarine, *C-3*, successfully blew a gap in the railroad viaduct, but the infantry landing was only partially successful. The problem was the mole itself. The top of the outer wall was twenty-five feet above the water, and the infantry had to climb rickety wooden ramps up from

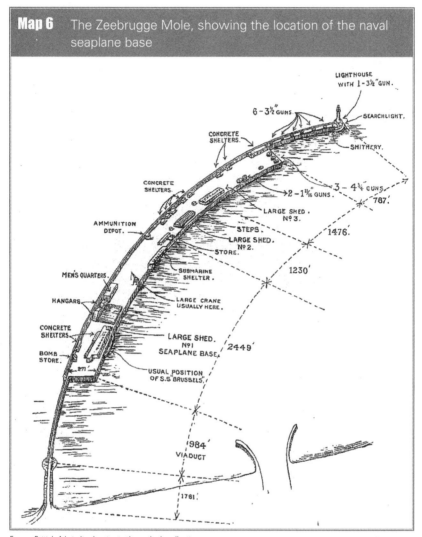

Map 6 The Zeebrugge Mole, showing the location of the naval seaplane base

From a British Admiralty drawing in the author's collection.

the *Vindictive*'s deck to the top of the mole wall in the face of murderous fire from small arms, machine guns, and heavy-caliber guns from two German destroyers laid alongside the mole floor.

At 12:50 a.m., while the battle raged on the mole, the three block ships—HMS *Thetis*, HMS *Intrepid*, and HMS *Iphigenia*—rounded the end of the mole at the lighthouse and immediately came under heavy fire from the shore batteries. The *Thetis* was hit several times and grounded well away from the canal entrance, but the *Intrepid* and *Iphigenia* reached the canal entrance and scuttled themselves. British motor launches recovered the crews of the three block ships, the British infantry fought their way back to the *Vindictive*, and the entire force pulled away shortly before 2 a.m. on 23 April.

British casualties, mostly infantry, were put at two hundred dead and three hundred wounded, though the numbers were probably higher; fifty were captured. The goal of the raid, to block the canal entrance, was only partially achieved, and then for just two days. The two block ships did not fully block the entrance, and the room left on each side of the channel was sufficient at high water to allow the UB and UC boats to pass through. Additional dredging and the removal of two piers widened the opening even more, and the Marinekorps continued to send U-boats to sea in the same numbers as prior to the raid.[10]

Killinger distinguished himself during the defense of the seaplane base, which he organized and led. In May 1918 he received the Hohenzollern House Order, Honor Cross, Third Class with Swords and Crown, for his actions.

After failing to block the channel entrances, the British stepped up air attacks on Zeebrugge and Ostend in an attempt to damage or destroy the outer lock gates. The increase in air raids kept the Seeflugstation I fighters very busy, and Killinger probably saw his share of combat during those raids.

In July 1918 Killinger was a pallbearer for Karl von Gorrissen's funeral. Von Gorrissen had been released from his POW camp in January 1918 following the Russian Revolution and returned to Germany. He was promoted to Kapitänleutnant zur See on 17 March 1918, backdated to 26 April 1917, and was assigned to a naval aviation unit at Warnemünde. On 17 July 1918 he was the commanding officer at the Naval Air Station Putzig when he took off on a routine patrol. When he was about a nautical mile off the Isle of Sylt, his engine quit and his plane crashed into the North Sea. His body was recovered, and the naval funeral was held at the Isle of Sylt Naval Air Station.

The Marinekorps evacuation of Flanders began on 28 September following a meeting on 16 and 17 September with Admiral Reinhard Scheer, chief of the Naval Staff, and Admiral Ludwig von Schröder, commanding officer of the Marinekorps Flandern, in Bruges, at which Admiral Scheer told von Schröder that Bruges had to be evacuated. The evacuation started the following day and included all Marinekorps forces except those committed to holding the German army's right flank.

Between 18 September and 3 October all the surface warships were withdrawn to bases in Germany. On 4 October the Allies launched an offensive into Flanders and the Germans started destroying the harbor facilities in Bruges, Zeebrugge, and Ostend. On 5 October the German chancellor, Georg Michaelis, announced in the Reichstag that he had asked President Woodrow Wilson to bring about "the immediate conclusion of an armistice on land, water, and in the air."[11] It was now obvious that the war was winding down. On 21 October 1918 the German Admiralty ordered all U-boats at sea to "return immediately. During the return passage all forms of antishipping warfare are forbidden. Encountered enemy submarines and warships may be attacked only during daytime."

All the U-boats in Bruges, Zeebrugge, and Ostend that were capable of making the trip to Germany were sent home as they became ready. Those that could not make the trip were destroyed in place. After the evacuation of the U-boats, the Marinekorps seaplanes were flown back to Germany. The destruction of the harbors and remaining U-boats continued until 18 October. Admiral von Schröder left Bruges on the morning of 17 October, and the remaining troops departed during the night of 18 October.[12]

On 29 October, when the High Seas Fleet was ordered to sea in a final battle of glory and death, the enlisted crews mutinied and Germany collapsed into revolution, rioting, and civil war.[13] On 10 November 1918 Oberleutnant zur See Hellmuth von Doemming in *UB-67* torpedoed the 810-ton paddlewheel minesweeper HMS *Ascot* off the Northumberland coast near the Farne Islands. His was the last torpedo fired in World War I.[14] The following day Germany signed the Armistice.

Killinger was with his unit in Kiel when the war ended. He was released from duty on 24 November 1919, recalled on 19 December, promoted to Leutnant zur See on 7 January 1920, and finally discharged on 9 March 1920. The discharge ended his naval career.

During the interwar period he became an international representative for various German and British aircraft and engine manufacturers. From 1920 to 1923 he was a salesman in Java, Sumatra, China, and Japan for a group of German aviation companies. He returned to Germany in 1924 and was unemployed for a year before he retraced his escape route in reverse, starting in New York and traveling west across the United States. He went by ship to Shanghai and then by train to Harbin. From there he rode the Trans-Siberian Railway to Leningrad, formerly St. Petersburg, and then went by ship to Flensburg.

In 1926 he became a representative for Junkers in Madrid, a position he held for three years, during which he partnered with Union Aeria Hispaniola and Servizios Portugesis in establishing two airlines.[15] When he returned to Germany from Spain in 1929, he went to work for the British aircraft engine manufacturer Armstrong-Siddeley Motors as the company's general manager in Berlin. He was with Armstrong-Siddeley on 11 April 1930 when he married Thea Margot Schroeder, a German national who had been born in London. Erich was thirty-nine and Thea was thirty-one. They had three children: Klaus, born on 19 January 1931; Karin, born 1 October 1937; and Erich, born on 20 February 1939.

Shortly after he married Thea, he took a government position in the Reichsluftfahrtministerium (Empire Aviation Ministry) as the director of the Wirtschaftsgruppe Luftfahrtindustrie (Economic Group Aviation Industry). It was a position with a promising future until 30 January 1933, when Adolf Hitler was named chancellor. Almost immediately Killinger's position put him into direct conflict with the "New Order." The Nazis were consolidating their power by merging government agencies and purging them of executive-level jobholders who were not party members. Killinger was not a member and refused to join, so he was fired.

Other than losing his job, Killinger suffered no further pressures from the Nazis, who ignored him until eight years later. He did not remain unemployed very long and soon founded his own industrial organization, the Aussenhandelsabteilung Wirtschaftsgruppe des Reichsverbandes der deutschen Luftfahrtindustrie (Foreign Commerce Division of the Empire Association of the German Aviation Industry) in Berlin.[16]

In 1938 he applied for a Luftwaffe commission and was commissioned a major in the Luftwaffe Reserve. It was not uncommon at the time for a former naval officer to become a Luftwaffe officer. In some cases the switch was political, the former naval officer having become a Nazi Party member; Killinger simply had a strong attachment to aviation. With war imminent, he was called up on 1 August 1939.

His first wartime assignment was on the staff of Coastal Aviation Group 506, which was based at Pillau in East Prussia on the Baltic. The group was equipped with Heinkel HE-59 and HE-60 seaplanes, which in many respects were not much different from the Rumpler he and von Gorrissen had flown in 1915. Both were fabric-covered biplanes used for aerial reconnaissance at sea. The Heinkel HE-59 was a twin-engine floatplane whose four-man crew rode in open cockpits, and the HE-60 was a single-engine floatplane with a two-man crew who also rode in open cockpits. Being stationed on the Baltic was also like a step back in time.

Group 506 was the closest Killinger could get to a naval aviation unit because in the Reich the navy had no air arm, all aviation being in Hermann Göring's Luftwaffe. Though Group 506 was a Luftwaffe unit, it included naval officers among its personnel, usually as observers. The group cooperated with the German navy and at a later date came under navy control, but it always remained a Luftwaffe unit.

Killinger remained with Group 506, taking part in the Polish campaign and flying regular missions, until he left in July 1940 to join the staff of the Luftwaffe headquarters in France, a nonflying assignment that he did not like. In March 1941 he managed to get reassigned to Coastal Aviation Group 506, but that assignment lasted just eight months. On 15 November 1941, now an Oberstleutnant (lieutenant colonel), he was given command of a POW camp at Oberursel near Frankfurt am Main.

WAR CRIMINAL

The Germans opened Dulag Luft in December 1939 as an interrogation center exclusively for Allied airmen who were captured in occupied Europe, Germany, and Austria, with the collateral purpose of being a transit camp (*dulag* is a contraction of *Durchgangslager*, or "transit camp"). The interrogation center was expanded on 26 August 1939 to include Hohemark, a prewar civilian clinic that became the camp hospital, and in April 1940 a much larger building was constructed to be the aircrew interrogation center called Auswertestelle West. With the addition of the new, dedicated interrogation center, Dulag Luft became just a transit camp. But despite the expansion into three separate units—the transit camp, Dulag Luft; the interrogation center, Auswertestelle West; and the hospital, Hohemark—the prisoners who passed through called the entire complex Dulag Luft, and the name stuck.

The camp's first commanding officer was Luftwaffe Oberstleutnant (Lieutenant Colonel) Peterpaul von Donat, a member of the SA—the brown-shirt thugs who were the Nazi Party's muscle before 1933. His time in command was very short; before the month was out Major Theodor Rumpel replaced him.[1]

Rumpel was a World War 1 fighter ace who flew in Jasta 26 with Hermann Göring from 18 March until 22 April 1917, when he went to Jasta 16. He scored his first two victories while flying in that unit and was awarded the Iron Cross, First Class. He joined Jasta 23 on 17 September 1917, scoring the three victories that raised his status to ace. He was still flying with Jasta 23 when he was shot down and seriously wounded on 24 March 1918.[2]

Between the wars Rumpel represented German business interests in Holland and the Dutch East Indies. He returned to Germany in 1936 and was reactivated and assigned to the Luftwaffe General Staff in the intelligence section that dealt with foreign air forces (Abteilung für fremde Luftmächte). He was promoted to Hauptmann (captain) in 1938 and to Major in 1939.[3]

Rumpel was forty-four years old when he relieved von Donat. He was a genial man who spoke three languages fluently—Dutch, English, and Malay (Bashasa Melayu)—and those who knew him described him as engaging and courteous. He reinstituted the World War I practice of allowing officer prisoners to accept chaperoned parole for excursions outside the wire. Dulag Luft prisoners took strolls in the forests around the camp, often joined Rumpel for dinner, and on occasion even went skiing. Despite Rumpel's enlightened management style, seventeen prisoners made the first mass escape in World War II from Dulag Luft on the night of 1–2 June 1941. Squadron Leader Roger Bushell (famous today for leading the Great Escape at Stalag Luft III in 1944) led the escape through a tunnel that ran from the western barracks block and under a guard tower on the camp's southwestern corner. All were recaptured.

That was the only recorded escape attempt from Dulag Luft. Frankfurt Gestapo chief Klaus Bräder saw to that. He was already peeved at what he considered Rumpel's excessively kind treatment of the POWs, and the escape of seventeen prisoners was the final straw. On the grounds that he was too lenient and security was too lax, Rumpel was relieved of command on 15 November 1941. Bräder's dissatisfaction may not have been the only factor in Rumpel's dismissal. The Luftwaffe's intelligence section in Berlin was not satisfied with the sort of information Rumpel was sending them. The exact nature of the problem is not recorded, but the absence of technical information about enemy aircraft, plans, and strategy was likely a factor.

Oberstleutnant Erich Killinger was selected as Rumpel's replacement, and Bräder and the Luftwaffe command in Berlin initially felt he was the right man for the job. By all appearances he was a good choice; his qualifications were top notch. He had been a prisoner of war, which presumably gave him greater insight into dealing with POWs; and he had successfully escaped, which presumably gave him greater insight into camp security. He was a pilot and had worked for the German aircraft industry, so he had technical competence when it came to dealing with fliers, and he still spoke excellent English. And he had a reputation as a stickler for discipline that appealed to both the Luftwaffe and the Gestapo.

Air Vice-Marshal Ronald Ivelaw-Chapman, an air commodore and the senior RAF officer in the camp, later wrote that Killinger "was a strict disciplinarian with his subordinates and was generally unpopular with the men under him due to his free use of a very sarcastic tongue when issuing orders and criticizing their work . . . [and] was a martinet who drove his people hard. But his subordinates, even when they complained about him, always expressed high regard for his principles and general standard of ethics."[4]

A British officer who interrogated Killinger while he was being held in the London Cage in May and June 1945 offered another view of his character and style:

> We judge Killinger to be an extremely able officer well selected for his job, possessing a master mind at intrigue, most economical with the truth, and determined to win any battle where wits are the main weapons. It is quite reasonable to assume that he personally did not participate in handling POWs, but it would be wrong to suggest that he is not fully aware of all the important information obtained in Dulag Luft, and he appraised its value by knowledge of how it was obtained.[5]

Whatever the methods he employed, Killinger brought Auswertestelle West to peak efficiency while retaining many of Rumpel's practices regarding special privileges for selected prisoners, such as special outings, which he believed made them more cooperative. He repeatedly expressed his opinion that civilized behavior and treatment would yield more information than physical force. But his definition of civilized behavior and treatment was not quite as broad as Rumpel's had been, and some decidedly uncivilized behavior went on inside Auswertestelle West. Nevertheless, conditions in the interrogation center and the transit camp were much better than in any other German POW camp.

As the war progressed, Gestapo chief Bräder became increasingly dissatisfied with how Killinger was running the interrogation center. One of his chief complaints was that many prisoners who could not prove they were Allied air crewmen through official identification, such as the British identity disc and the American dog tag, were not being turned over to the Gestapo as regulations required.

Bräder had reason to be angry on that point. Hundreds of prisoners arrived at the center in civilian clothing, without identity discs and carrying false identity cards given to them by escape organizations in Belgium and Holland. Leutnant Herbert Boettner, the camp adjutant, described the situation in more detail:

> That happened every day. There was always one among the newcomers who tried to get into a camp run by the Luftwaffe, which was supposed to be much better than those for the army. Prisoners of war who escaped from army camps tried to get in under the pretext of having been shot down the day before, and there were many slave workers who had run away who tried to get in under the guise of being an air force prisoner of war. They were easily found out when we asked such questions as, "What is your name, rank, and serial number and to which unit did you belong?" The answer was usually something like, "I belonged to the First Bomber Group equipped with Hurricanes at Croydon." It was just a joke. Anybody who knew anything about airplanes knew that a Hurricane was a fighter, not a bomber, and Croydon does not belong to the RAF. So they were discovered through a simple question.

The civilian imposters were turned over to the Gestapo, but Killinger made every effort to retain control of military POWs regardless of whether or not they were aviators.

In 1944 Bräder tried to bring Killinger before a People's Court on charges of weakening the war effort. A British Air Ministry weekly intelligence summary dated 12 November 1945 reported: "In the autumn 1944, the Sicherheitsdienst office at Frankfurt charged Oberstleutnant Killinger and his interrogation officers with Anglophile tendencies, defeatism, and transgression of Service rules. The SS demanded punishment of the offenders and subordination to the SS of the prisoner of war interrogation center." Hermann Göring blocked the move and brought Killinger before a Luftwaffe court-martial that acquitted him.

But Killinger's supervisory style apparently encouraged some of his interrogators to go beyond the bounds of proper conduct, and the responsibility came to rest on his shoulders. From 26 November to 3 December 1945 a British military tribunal in Wuppertal, Germany, tried Killinger and four of his subordinates—Heinz Junge, Otto Boehringer, Heinrich Eberhardt, and Gustav Bauer-Schlichtegroll—for war crimes. Sir Frank Soskice detailed the charges in his foreword to *The Dulag Luft Trial*:

> They were charged with offences well established in international and municipal law and not with vaguer crimes

of offences against humanity or crimes against peace. The main accusations related to endeavors to extract operational information from Allied airmen by torture, namely by overheating the cells in which they were confined and by threats to hand them over to the Gestapo.

Specifically they were charged with: Committing a war crime in that you at or near Oberursel, Germany, between 1st November 1941 and 15th April 1945, when members of the staff of the Luftwaffe Interrogation Centre known as Dulag Luft, in violation of the laws and usages of war were together concerned as parties to the ill-treatment of British prisoners of war.

There were five specifications:

1. The electric heating of the cell was turned on to its maximum with the window and door shut and left on for hours at a stretch in order to cause the greatest possible discomfort to the prisoner.
2. Prisoners were threatened that if they did not vouchsafe the information demanded they would be handed over to the Gestapo and probably shot since if a prisoner did not answer fully he might be a saboteur.
3. In some cases a refusal of medical treatment, when medical care was necessary, until the questions had been answered.
4. Prolonged solitary confinement.
5. In a very few cases the administering of blows.

However, the prosecution limited the specifications to be proved to numbers 1, 3, and 5.

Major Heinz Junge was fifty-three at the time of the trial. He had been Killinger's second in command and was the chief interrogator at Auswertestelle West. Junge had been an artillery officer from 1911 to 1914 before transferring to aviation in August 1914 as an observer. He was wounded three times and finally shot down and taken prisoner by the French in February 1918. He was released in 1919 and went to Argentina, where he worked for a time for the Argentine government as a "commercial traveler" before taking the same position with the Peruvian government. He married a woman in Argentina, and in 1932 he joined the Nationalsozialistische Deutsche Arbeiterpartei (NSDAP, National Socialist German Workers Party), and became the South American representative for the German aviation industry.

In 1938 he was back in Germany working as the director of the Focke-Wulf office in Berlin. In that capacity he was on board the four-engine FW 200 IV Condor *Brandenburg* when it made a record-setting flight from Berlin to Tokyo in November 1938. He was also on board when the airplane crashed in Manila Bay on the return trip.

In 1941 Junge obtained a commission in the Luftwaffe and was sent back to South America to be the assistant air attaché in Buenos Aires. The Argentine government refused to recognize him, however, and he spent the next six months as an Abwehr (German army intelligence) agent in Argentina. He returned to Germany in 1942 to take the job as head of the interrogation department at Auswertestelle West because Killinger, who had formed a friendship with him before the war, had requested him. Junge came to the trial with strong endorsements from two men who had spent time in the interrogation center as POWs: Air Vice-Marshal Ronald Ivelaw-Chapman and Wing Commander Eric Douglas Elliot, who had been a prisoner in Dulag Luft from October 1940 to February 1944 and was the senior British officer from June 1941 to February 1944.

Major Otto Boehringer was fifty years old at the time of his trial and the owner of a Manheim factory that manufactured hydrants, water flow meters, and oil pressure meters. A Hauptmann in the army reserve before the war, he was called up in August 1939 and given command of a barrage balloon company until May 1940, when he was released from service and returned home to manage his factory. He and Killinger were longtime friends who had met in Java in the 1920s and developed a strong friendship that lasted through World War II and included their families. In November 1942 he learned that Killinger was the commandant at Dulag Luft and went there to visit his old friend, and Killinger urged him to return to active service and work with him at the interrogation center. Boehringer accepted the offer on the condition that he would be allowed to return to Manheim two days each week to look after his factory.

Boehringer conducted interrogations for a short time but was unsuited for that work and was "given various minor duties that varied from week to week and month to month." Actually, Boehringer's position was a sinecure—a job created for an old friend. During the trial several witnesses testified that they had no idea what his job was and that few people even knew him. He seems to have spent most of his time as the mess secretary and showing visitors around the camp, but he was nevertheless promoted to Major on 1 July 1943.

Leutnant Heinrich Eberhardt was thirty-six at the time of the trial and had been a secondary school teacher from 1932 to 1933. He joined the NSDAP on 1 May 1933 and studied English at the University of London in 1933 and 1934 before taking a position teaching in a secondary school in Darmstadt in 1934. He went to the University of Giessen as a lecturer in 1936 and stayed on until November 1939, then went to Dulag Luft in December 1939 as a civilian censoring mail. He was made a Luftwaffe Sonderführer in August 1940.

Luftwaffe Sonderführer was a temporary rank between noncommissioned officer (NCO) and commissioned officer held while the person was being trained in a technical specialty, in Eberhardt's case military intelligence. He was commissioned as a Leutnant in 1943. Before he was commissioned in 1943 Eberhardt was one of the camp receptionists—the officers who made the initial contact with newly arrived prisoners. His primary job was to have the prisoners fill out what was ostensibly an International Red Cross (IRC) form, but it asked for information far beyond the name, rank, and serial number that a prisoner is obliged to give. The bogus Red Cross form asked for the prisoner's home address, marital status, children, squadron number and station, type of aircraft he was in, and aircraft identification number, and then went into increasingly greater detail. Since his job was to get the prisoner to fill out the bogus IRC form, he often wore what looked like an IRC uniform. Eberhardt's task was to get the prisoners to answer as many questions as possible without actually interrogating them. In fact, until he was commissioned he was "expressly forbidden" to interrogate prisoners.

Gustav Bauer-Schlichtegroll was thirty-six at the time of the trial. He had learned English from his British nanny, which implies that he came from a fairly well-to-do family. In 1930, when he was nineteen, he was in London "working on patents regarding fluid transmissions on Daimler cars," and he made frequent trips to England through 1935. He joined the staff at Dulag Luft on 1 October 1941 as a civilian employee of the German Air Ministry and joined the Luftwaffe as a Sonderführer on 22 February 1942. He remained assigned to Auswertestelle West until the end of March 1945, when he apparently walked off the job and went home to his wife and parents in Kronberg, near Oberursel, where the British arrested him in June 1945.

Bauer-Schlichtegroll was an interrogator "of crews that dropped agents and saboteurs as well as materials for the underground movements." Though he was never a member of the NSDAP, he had frequent contact with the Gestapo and often traveled throughout Germany and occupied Europe to question prisoners whom the Gestapo had in custody. Of the five defendants, only Bauer-Schlichtegroll should not have been in that courtroom. He had an airtight alibi. On the dates laid out in the charges he was absent from Auswertestelle West, and at times he was not even in Germany. And he had the records to prove it.

The prosecution charged that deliberate overheating of the cells to make prisoners talk occurred six times from 16 to 19 May 1943, though there were several complaints about overheating at other times in 1943 and 1944. Eight witnesses gave testimony that the cells were overheated to make them talk, but only seven complained exclusively about the overheating. Of the seven whose testimony focused exclusively on the overheating charge, three gave their testimony in court and four gave their testimony in affidavits that were read to the court.

The first overheating witness was Warrant Officer Robert T. Lang, whose bomber was shot down on 1 April 1943 east of Amsterdam. He suffered bruises, shock, and a broken finger in the crash. He spent two weeks in a Dutch hospital, where a doctor set his finger, before arriving in Auswertestelle West on 15 May. The first person he met was Eberhardt, who came into his cell dressed as an IRC officer and tried to get Lang to fill out the bogus IRC form. When Lang refused to provide anything other than his name, rank, and serial number, Eberhardt yelled at him in a high voice, "You're a bloody fool!" and left the cell.

Lang described his cell as "approximately six by twelve feet with a sealed window of glazed glass. The door was built up in sections, so when it was shut it was perfectly airtight. The walls were of some sort of asbestos, I think. There was one bed with six bed-boards, a mattress, two sheets and blankets, a table, and a radiator approximately eight or nine inches in diameter, about four feet long, fastened halfway up from the floor to the window. The window was shut. As a matter of fact it was bolted all the time."

Lang told the court that after Eberhardt left, the next thing he heard was a "switching noise" from outside, and the radiator began to "vibrate." The temperature in the room became so "intense" that he had to strip to his undershorts and lie on the floor. After a while he got up and lay on the bed for about an hour. The heat, which he thought had been turned up at about 10 or 10:30 a.m., was turned off at about 2 p.m. when he was allowed to go down the hall to use the toilet. He told the court that though there was a heat wave outside, the air in the corridor was cool. He was returned to his cell and saw no one for the rest of the day. The next day a sergeant medical orderly visited, and Lang asked to see a doctor. Instead the sergeant examined Lang's bandaged arm and finger and left. Shortly after that a different Luftwaffe officer came in and questioned him briefly about his squadron and "other service matters." When Lang refused to answer his questions, the officer left, saying that he would keep Lang there for fourteen days. Immediately after the German left, the heat came on again and remained on for five hours. Lang said that he stripped and lay on his bed, "feeling pretty grim" due to the pain in his arm and finger.

The same officer returned after the heat had been turned off and again asked Lang questions about his squadron, which Lang answered this time. The officer left and the heat was not turned on again. Lang's answers under cross-examination were generally consistent, although he confused Eberhardt with the second officer who questioned him.

The second overheating witness was Lang's pilot, Squadron Leader James Campbell Cairns. He told the court that he was flying a Wellington bomber when he was shot down on 26 April 1943, which did not match Lang's testimony that he was shot down on 1 April. It was a small difference but possibly speaks to Lang's occasionally confused and contradictory testimony under cross-examination.

Cairns' testimony was similar to Lang's, though it differed slightly on specific points. His clothes, except for his undershorts, were taken from him when he and Lang arrived in the center on 15 May, and he was placed in a cell alone. Two days later Eberhardt, wearing the uniform of a Luftwaffe Sonderführer, came into the cell, returned Cairns' clothes, and handed him the Red Cross form to fill out. Cairns testified that he filled in the blanks for his name, rank, and serial number "but left blank the other questions dealing with marriage, location of squadron, group, command, and so on, which were obviously not of any use to the Red Cross." As Eberhardt left the cell, he called to the guard and closed the door. Cairns heard two men speaking in German and then the sound of a switch being turned. Nothing happened for five minutes, and then the cell started to become uncomfortably warm.

Cairns knocked on the door and told the guard who opened it that he wanted to see an officer. Shortly, a different interrogator arrived, and Cairns told him the cell was becoming too warm. The officer said he would see to it and left, but the heat remained on. "It got hotter and extremely difficult to breathe," Cairns testified; "the metal-work on the bed got to such a temperature that it was too hot to touch, and I perspired freely all over my body. Perspiration was dripping from my nose, chin, and hands pretty quickly."

The heat remained on for about two and a half hours. At 1 p.m. the officer to whom Cairns had complained returned and turned it off while the guard opened the cell window, allowing the room to "cool down quickly." At the close of his direct examination Cairns made a correct in-court identification of Eberhardt.

The third witness was Warrant Officer Norman Rees, a flight engineer whose Lancaster bomber was shot down near Duisberg, Germany, on the night of 13 May 1943. He evaded capture for two nights while he walked into Holland, where he went to a farmhouse hoping to find something to eat. The people in the house fed him but also called the local police, who turned him over to the Germans. From there he went to Dulag Luft via Amsterdam.

When he arrived at the interrogation center his clothes were taken from him and he was placed in a cell. The following day Eberhardt came to his cell wearing a "white uniform jacket" and claiming to be from the International Red Cross. He handed Rees the fake IRC form and asked him to fill it out. Rees filled in his name, rank, and serial number and returned the form to Eberhardt. Seeing that the remaining blanks were empty, Eberhardt "raved" and warned Rees that he might be turned over to the Gestapo and shot. He then left the cell.

Shortly after Eberhardt left, Rees was taken an office where a different officer asked him several questions that Rees refused to answer. That afternoon he was moved to another cell, and the following morning the temperature began to rise. Rees called the guard and told him the radiator was on, but the guard only laughed "as if he did not understand" and closed the door. Rees thought the heat remained on for about ten hours. He told the court: "It was very hot. I would have collapsed except for the fact that I lay on the floor and breathed some of the cool air that came under the door. I had taken everything off and was naked. I lay on the floor in a pool of my own perspiration with my face right down at the bottom where the floor adjoined the door. Practically everything in the cell was too hot to touch, the thing I noticed particularly being the bed rail, which was very hot and which I could not keep hold of."

At about 6 p.m. that evening the second, unnamed officer came to the cell and, finding it very hot, called a guard whom he "appeared to tell off." The officer asked Rees if he was ready to answer the questions, and Rees replied that he would if he was removed from the hot cell. That was done and Rees told the officer what he wanted to know.

The first of the four affidavits dealing with the overheating charge were then read to the court. The first affidavit was by Warrant Officer Pilot Victor Albert Bain, who was flying a Beaufighter off Norway when he was shot down at sea on 1 May 1943. He and his back-seater, Sgt. Cecil Albert Room, were adrift in their life rafts until the following day when a Luftwaffe three-engine DO24 landed on the water, took them on board, and flew them to Stavanger. He and Sergeant Room were separated and transferred individually to Auswertestelle West, where Bain arrived on 8 May.

Bain testified that on the day he arrived an unidentified man wearing civilian clothes came into his cell. Bain described him as "tall, of medium build, clean shaven, and with dark hair turning gray." He estimated the man's age at about fifty, adding that he spoke excellent English. The man took Bain's name, rank, and serial number before launching into a conversation about the Beaufighter, about which he seemed well informed. The conversation turned to Bain's Beaufighter wing, which had been recently formed and had just begun operations. The man was particularly interested in Bain and his observer because they were the first members of the new wing that the Germans had captured.

That line of interrogation lasted seven consecutive days before the heat in Bain's cell was turned up. By noon the heat was "almost unbearable. It was so hot that it was impossible to put one's hand on the bed frame." By 2 p.m. Bain felt that he could not bear it any longer and asked for "his interrogation officer." A different officer showed up with the fake Red Cross form. Bain refused to fill it out and demanded that the heat be turned off. When the German told him that "the heating system had gone wrong," Bain became so enraged at the blatant lie that he balled his fists and shouted, "If you don't get out of here I'll punch your bloody head!" The German quickly left, bolting the door behind him.

> I then tried to get relief by undressing and sponging myself with the water I had used for washing that morning. But that also had become so warmed that it afforded no relief. I lay on my bed for two hours or so, at the end of which time one of my arms dropped over the side of the bed and I noticed that near the floor it seemed not quite so hot. I got up and investigated and found that the door at the bottom did not fit quite closely and by lying on the floor and putting my mouth to the crack I could get a little cool air. By remaining in that position I obtained a measure of relief to the bodily and mental strain, which had become almost unendurable.

Bain did not know when the heat was finally turned off, but the following day the original interrogator showed up and apologized to Bain about the hot room. He showed Bain a list of airfields that were correctly marked and asked him to show his movements, not including his last airfield. Bain complied because the airfield names were already correct, so he was not telling the German anything he did not already know. He remained in the cell with the heat turned off until the end of his second week in the interrogation center, when he was moved with a large prisoner contingent to Stalag Luft I at Barth.

The second affidavit read was that of Warrant Officer John Gale, whose B-25 ran into flak and went down on 13 May 1943 on the French coast near Boulogne. He and his copilot, Flying Officer I. Twedell, were the only two who successfully bailed out. Antiaircraft troops captured them both, and they arrived in Auswertestelle West on 15 May.

On 16 May "a young man dressed in a neutral uniform, grey trousers, tunic, and peaked cap without badges" entered Gale's cell carrying a Red Cross form. Gale described the man as "young and fair"; he spoke fluent English with a slight German accent. Two days later an older man, fifty-five to sixty and wearing civilian clothes, came to the cell and opened a conversation about politics. He soon shifted to asking Gale his squadron number and other military questions. When Gale refused to answer, the man warned him, "Well Mr. Gale, you will not stick it out," and left.

Within a few minutes of his leaving the cell the heating came on. I knew it was deliberate so I did not call the guard to turn it off. It was so strong that when standing upright I could not breathe properly. I lay on the bed, from which the mattress had been removed. There were only the bed-boards to lie on. Sweat poured off me. I then lay on the floor and tried to breathe cool air through a gap of a quarter of an inch under the door. The metal of my trouser buttons and braces became too hot for the skin on my forearm. I put a piece of wood shaving that had fallen out of the mattress onto the radiator and within three seconds it curled up black.

The heat remained on until 11 p.m., when the guard came to collect his boots, as was done every evening. Gale estimated that the heat had been on for ten and a half hours.

The third affidavit came from Warrant Officer Pilot Gerald Marcel Clarke, who was over Ostend on 14 May 1943 when his Spitfire was shot down and he bailed out. Other than sustaining bruises and cuts, he was unwounded. He arrived at the interrogation center on 18 May and refused to provide more than his name, rank, and serial number. The interrogator warned him that if he did not answer the questions, "he would be shot as a spy." Clarke was kept in the cell for two weeks, on ten days of which the heat was turned up for "short periods each day," the longest period being "not more than an hour." He said that while the heat was on the room became "uncomfortable" and it was "necessary to strip."

The fourth affidavit came from Flying Lieutenant William Dudley Cassini Hawkes, who described a completely different set of circumstances than the others described. Hawkes was forced to bail out over Italy on 20 November 1944 when the engine of his Spitfire abruptly stopped running. He suffered a very painful left knee injury when he jumped. The Germans first took him to Verona, and from there he went to Auswertestelle West, arriving on 25 November.

Following his refusal to fill out more than his name, rank, and serial number on the Red Cross form, he was placed in what he called the "sweat box"—a small room with twenty American airmen all seated on stools. Hawkes described the room as "blacked-out and not ventilated at all; the temperature was very high." He remained in the room for two hours and was then moved to a cell. On the second day he was taken to the Hohemark hospital, where his knee injury was treated.

Boehringer's defense consul, Maj. C. J. Rickard, made sure the record showed that when Major Otto Boehringer heard about the overheating he immediately reported it to Junge, who in turn told Killinger. On the following day Killinger issued an order that the heaters were not to be turned on "at all" during the summer. He took no further action in the matter and made no attempt to identify the interrogators who were involved.

During the trial, the prosecution tried to establish that the heaters installed in the cells were chosen because they were much too powerful for the job. Because Killinger was in charge of the new construction at Auswertestelle West in early 1943, the prosecution alleged that he had the powerful heaters installed for the purpose of "torturing" the prisoners to make them talk.

Jacob Ackermann, a German civilian who worked for the company that installed the heaters, refuted that, saying that they were all standard Luftwaffe issue that he drew from the Luftwaffe supply center in Frankfurt. Capt. Werner G. Walker, USA Corps of Engineers, testified after Ackerman. Walker was the engineer in charge of maintaining Auswertestelle West after U.S. Army intelligence took over the center for the interrogation of suspected war criminals. He said that the heaters the Germans had installed in the center during the war were actually understrength for the job of heating the complex during winter, and he had replaced them with bigger heaters.

The direct testimony and affidavits established that instances of overheating the cells to make prisoners answer various questions had occurred on several occasions, including several times outside the dates specified in the allegation. Killinger admitted that the overheating occurred, and Junge provided the names of men he thought might have done it, among them Bauer-Schlichtegroll.

The second allegation was that medical treatment had been withheld from wounded prisoners who arrived at the interrogation center to force them to talk. To support the allegation the prosecution called on three in-court witnesses and submitted one affidavit.

The first witness called was Company Sergeant-Major Alfred Alexander Brown, who landed on D-day with the Royal Warwickshire Regiment.

He was captured near Caen on 9 June after he was shot twice in the left thigh and was unable to walk. The Germans took him to a field dressing station where his wounds were treated, and from there he went to a Luftwaffe hospital in Paris, where he remained as a bed case for two weeks. He was taken by train to Auswertestelle West along with one British and three American airmen. The reason the Germans sent him to an interrogation center that was exclusively for Allied airmen is a simple matter of German bureaucracy—he was in a Luftwaffe hospital, ergo he was an airman.

Company Sergeant-Major Brown told the court that during the train trip from Paris he "suffered grave discomfort. . . . My wounds had been healing up, but as I had to hobble across the station to the train, by the time I reached Frankfurt one of the wounds, a gash about six inches long, was gaping wide open and bleeding."

Upon his arrival at the interrogation center he was taken to an office where a Luftwaffe officer, whom he said "was very sympathetic" about his condition, assured him that his wounds would be treated. There followed several questions about Brown's unit during which the officer asked Brown what the unit insignia on his shoulders meant. When Brown refused to tell him, the officer showed him a binder that contained illustrations of British regimental insignias and pointed out the insignia of the Royal Warwickshire Regiment, saying, "You see, we know all about you." When Brown continued to refuse to provide any information beyond his name, rank, and serial number, the officer said that he would be taken to a cell and kept without medical treatment until he answered the questions. Brown told the court that the officer was Bauer-Schlichtegroll and then pointed him out in the courtroom.

In fact, Company Sergeant-Major Brown had never seen Bauer-Schlichtegroll during the three days he was held in Auswertestelle West because Bauer-Schlichtegroll was in France at that time. The first time Brown laid eyes on him was in the London Cage in Kensington Palace Garden in June 1945. On that occasion he viewed Bauer-Schlichtegroll in a one-man lineup and made a positive identification on the basis of the "unusual look in his eyes and partly by his voice." The next time he saw Bauer-Schlichtegroll was in the Wuppertal courtroom.

Flying Officer Maurice William George Collins was a radioman on a Lancaster bomber that was shot down on the night of 19 October 1944.

He bailed out at 20,000 feet and came down in trees. He released his parachute harness and fell to the ground, where he lay unconscious until the early hours of the morning. When he tried to move he experienced severe pain in his legs and stomach and lost consciousness again. He spent the day regaining and losing consciousness until dusk, when German soldiers found him.

When the defense asked the nature of his injuries he said, "I never have been able to ascertain my wounds, but I understand that it was wounds to the bones in my stomach and legs, and from my waist to about six inches from the tops of my legs I was completely black with bruises." He said that civilians and soldiers who moved him from place to place mishandled him, causing increased pain and frequent periods of unconsciousness. A doctor examined him in a hospital in Essinger, and from there he went by train to Frankfurt. During the train trip he received no medical treatment.

In the interrogation center an officer in a black uniform questioned him about his squadron and his fellow crewmen, and Collins refused to answer. Collins told the officer that something was wrong with his stomach, to which the officer replied, "Here we give medical treatment if you give answers." Collins said that during the three days he was in the cell he was questioned twice, and each time he asked for medical attention and was refused. On the third day he was moved to the Hohemark hospital, where he remained for eighteen days.

Flying Sergeant Albert Tom Barnes was shot down over Holland on the night of 23 September 1944. During the shoot-down and bailout he suffered a broken collarbone and a concussion. Sometime between his capture on 23 September and his arrival at Auswertestelle West, a Dutch doctor examined his shoulder but did not bind it, instead directing Barnes to put it "beneath his clothing."

Upon his arrival at the interrogation center Barnes was searched, fingerprinted, and placed in a cell but received no medical attention of any kind that night. Because the Germans who captured him took away his identity disc, the "Red Cross" officer he spoke with told him that he would have to provide proof that he was an RAF aircrew member and asked Barnes about his aircraft, mission, and his fellow crewmembers. Barnes refused to answer. The officer told him that he would probably be turned over to the Gestapo unless he could prove his "innocence," and gave him until 5:30 p.m. to think it over. When Barnes asked to have a doctor look at his shoulder, the officer said nothing.

Barnes testified that he "could not undress properly because my battle-dress blouse had been tied up with a string to keep it together and I could not untie the knot with one hand. I had on a flying sweater, which I could not pull off, and I had a concussion. I was very 'headachy' and when I lay down I could not get up because of the broken bone."

Making matters even worse, on the second and third days the heat was turned up in his cell. "I noticed that the room was getting very hot, so I went to the radiator and found that I could not bear to touch it. I could hardly breathe. This carried on until after I went to bed, because when I lay in bed I was still sweating and it was unbearable. I must have gone to sleep because when I woke up it was cold again." Because he was unable to undress himself, during the time the heat was on he was fully dressed.

The following day a different interrogator came to the cell and questioned Barnes about the raid, his aircraft, equipment, and especially radar. Barnes again refused to answer and was again threatened with being turned over to the Gestapo. Barnes asked again for medical attention, and the German told him that unless he answered the questions there would be no medical treatment. At that time Barnes' arm was still under his clothing, making it impossible to undress himself.

Eight days passed during which the same officer continued asking questions that Barnes refused to answer. Barnes repeatedly asked to have his shoulder treated, but he received no medical treatment of any kind during those eight days. A medical orderly did come to the cell every morning, and Barnes told him he had not yet been to the hospital. The orderly answered that Barnes had to "apply" to his interrogator, who would "fix it up." When he was questioned on the stand, Barnes said that the officer who interrogated him was not in the courtroom.

When Barnes received permission to go outside his cell to the toilet, he instead "ran in the other direction" to the Medical Inspection Room, where he found Oberarzt Dr. Ernst Ittershagen, the camp doctor. Doctor Ittershagen took one look at Barnes' shoulder and ordered him taken to the hospital immediately. Barnes received excellent care in Hohemark, but he was repeatedly interrogated in his room while he was there.

In his opening remarks at the trial, the prosecutor, Major G. T. D. Draper, told the members of the court that among the methods used in

Auswertestelle West to obtain information "were, in some cases, blows." This charge stemmed from an incident that involved Bauer-Schlichtegroll. Called to the stand, Bauer-Schlichtegroll described what happened:

> A prisoner of war escaped from the cell by smashing the window, cutting through an iron bar, and bending it back. He was recaptured and I went to his cell to reproach him for the damage to German property. I shouted at him and he said, "Get out of my room or I will chuck you out," and advanced toward me. I went into the corridor and called a guard to arrest the man immediately, and when the guard came forward the prisoner jumped on the bed and began raining blows on the guard, nearly knocking him out. I called another guard and together they managed to seize the man. I said, "Will you apologize now?" and he said, "Yes, I do." I reported the incident immediately to Colonel Killinger, who criticized me and said I should have left the cell, locked the prisoner in, and reported to him. I never heard of any official complaint from the prisoner. I do not think the prisoner was punished.

The prisoner was not identified, but based on his speech he was probably an American. In any event, he did not complain; otherwise his name would have been known.

On Monday 3 December 1945, the court closed at 12:20 p.m. to await the jury's decision. Three hours and forty minutes later the court reopened and the president of the court read the charge: "Committing a war crime in that you at or near Oberursel, Germany, between 1st November 1941 and 15th April 1945, when members of the staff of the Luftwaffe Interrogation Centre known as Dulag Luft, in violation of the laws and usages of war were together concerned as parties to the ill-treatment of British prisoners of war."

He then read the verdict:

> Erich Killinger, guilty
> Heinz Junge, guilty
> Heinrich Eberhardt, guilty
> Otto Boehringer, not guilty
> Gustav Bauer-Schlichtegroll, not guilty

Killinger and Junge were each sentenced to five years' imprisonment; Eberhardt received three years. None of the three defendants who were convicted served the full term of their sentences. Eberhardt was released in 1947, and Killinger and Junge were released in 1948.

From July 1950 until he retired in 1963 Killinger was a representative for Ütersener Maschinenfabrik Hatlapa near Hamburg, a manufacturer of ship's equipment such as auxiliary motors, cargo-handling equipment, anchor windlasses, and compressors. He died on 18 May 1977 in Grensbach, Baden, just a few miles southeast of Rastatt.[6]

Notes

A Comment on the Sources

In light of high publishing costs, I have tried to keep the source notes to a minimum while providing the reader with enough information to backtrack to historical sources. My primary sources are the four official reports that Killinger wrote following his return to Germany in March 1916 and the two books he ostensibly wrote about his experiences. Those are the only primary sources I know of that describe Killinger's capture, escape, and return to Germany.

Killinger's two books are essentially identical. The 1917 version, *Die Abenteuer des Ostseefliegers*, was written for a domestic wartime market during the time of Kaiser Wilhelm II and contains a few minor inaccuracies and omissions, mostly wartime propaganda portraying German officers as clever and the Russians as stupid. The 1934 version, *Flucht um die Erde*, is an expanded version of the 1917 book that contains the same inaccuracies and omissions but adds new "details" aimed at a National Socialist Market. I relied more heavily on the earlier version because I believe that it more accurately describes the events than the version the Nazis published.

Chapter 1. Erich Killinger

1. Erich Killinger, *Die Abenteuer des Ostseefliegers* (Berlin: Ullstein, 1917), 11–14.
2. "Erich Walter Emil Killinger Biografie" (provided by Klaus Liedtke, Bibliothek-Archiv, Marine-Offizier-Vereinigung, Ulrich-von-Hassell-Strasse 2, D-53123 Bonn, Germany); Killinger, *Die Abenteuer des Ostseefliegers*, 11–14.
3. "Crew IV/1913," a class roster and ship assignments, and "Eintrag, Erich Killinger," a service history, 1913–1945 (provided by Joachim Scherneck-Czech, Wehrgeschichtlichen Ausbildungszentrum der Marineschule Mürwik, Kelmstrasse 14 D-24944 Flensburg).

4. Rudolph Firle, *Der Krieg in der Ostsee*, vol. 1 (Berlin: Verlag E. S. Mittler & Sohn, 1921), 89, 177, 206, and table 3; Erich Gröner, *Die Deutschen Kriegsschiffe, 1815–1945*, vol. 1 (Munich: J. F. Lehmanns Verlag, 1966), 67–68; Otto Groos, *Der Krieg in der Nordsee*, vol. 1 (Berlin: Verlag E. S. Mittler & Sohn, 1922), 24.

5. John Howard Morrow Jr., *Building German Airpower, 1909–1914* (Knoxville: University of Tennessee Press, 1976), 88–93.

Chapter 2. Erich Goes to War

1. Bill Gunston, *World Encyclopedia of Aircraft Manufacturers* (Annapolis: Naval Institute Press, 1993); Morrow, *Building German Airpower*, 26–27, 30, 37, 61.

2. Todesanzeige, Karl von Gorrissen, *Marineforum* (February 1919) (provided by Holger Hoffmann, *Marineforum*, Organ der Marine-Offizier-Vereinigung, Bonn); Karl von Gorrissen, geb. 4 August 1888, "Flieger-Karteikarte"; *Ehrenrangliste der Kaiserlichen-Marine, 1914–1918*, Bibliothek für Zeitgeschichte, Stuttgart; "Personalunterlagen für Karl von Gorrissen," Deutsche Dienststelle für die Benachrichtigung der nächsten Angehörigen von Gefallenen der ehemaligen deutschen Wehrmacht, Berlin.

3. Rumpler Werke, *Rumpler: Zehn Jahre Deutsche Flugtechnik* (Berlin: Echsteins Biographischer Verlag, 1921), 102–3; Morrow, *Building German Airpower*, 93.

4. Paul G. Halpern, *A Naval History of World War I* (Annapolis: Naval Institute Press, 1994), 182; Firle, *Der Krieg in der Ostsee*, 1:4, 76.

5. Firle, *Der Krieg in der Ostsee*, 1:4, 76.

6. S. L. A. Marshall, *World War I* (New York: American Heritage Press, 1971), 94–107.

7. Firle, *Der Krieg in der Ostsee*, vol. 1. The account of using aircraft to bomb the Memel bridges is on pp. 130–31.

8. Halpern, *Naval History*, 180–82; Firle, *Der Krieg in der Ostsee*, 1:1–15.

9. Halpern, *Naval History*, 184.

10. Firle, *Der Krieg in der Ostsee*, 1:74.

11. Ibid., 227.

12. Ibid., 236–37.

13. Gröner, *Die Deutschen Kriegsschiffe*, 2:533; Dieter Jung, Berndt Wenzel, and Arno Abendroth, *Die Schiffe und Boote der deutschen Seeflieger*,

1912–1976 (Stuttgart: Motorbuch Verlag, 1977), 194–95; Heinrich Rollmann, *Der Krieg in der Ostsee*, vol. 2 (Berlin: E. S. Mittler & Sohn, 1929), 33; Erich Killinger, *Die Flucht um die Erde* (Berlin: Ullstein, 1934), 14–19.

14. Firle, *Der Krieg in der Ostsee*, 1:281–82.
15. Rollmann, *Der Krieg in der Ostsee*, 2:7–13.
16. Ibid., 33.
17. Ibid. The account of air operations at and around Memel is on pp. 33–35.

Chapter 3. Captured

1. "Bericht des Leutnants zur See Killinger über seine Gefangennahme in Russland und Flucht aus Siberien, 11 March 1916," typewritten report, Records of the German Navy, 1850–1945, RG242, microfilm publication T1022, rolls 657 and 658, PG75191, National Archives II, College Park, Md.; Killinger, *Die Abenteuer des Ostseefliegers*, 9–17. Unless otherwise noted, the account and quotations in this chapter are from these two sources.
2. Firle, *Der Krieg in der Ostsee*, 1:8.
3. Maj. Gen. Sir Alfred Knox, *With the Russian Army, 1914–1917: Being Chiefly Extracts from the Diary of a Military Attaché* (London: Hutchenson and Company, 1921), xxiii.
4. Killinger, *Die Abenteuer des Ostseefliegers*, 14. Based on what is written in both of Killinger's books, many historians say that Russian anti-aircraft fire (flak) shot the plane down. However, Killinger's official report written in March 1916 simply says that the propeller came off and mentions only small arms and machine-gun fire. He also describes a "knocking" noise in the engine prior to the propeller coming off. Both books were published as propaganda, so attributing the crash to enemy antiaircraft fire rather than a mechanical failure, which might imply shoddy construction or poor maintenance, would not be surprising. I have given more weight to Killinger's official report that says the propeller came off unexpectedly, implying a defective shaft.
5. Firle, *Der Krieg in der Ostsee*, 1:33.
6. Killinger, *Die Abenteuer des Ostseefliegers*, 15–17.
7. Firle, *Der Krieg in der Ostsee*, 1:33.

Chapter 4. The First Escape Attempt

1. "Bericht des Leutnants zur See Killinger über seine Gefangennahme in Russland und Flucht aus Siberien, 11 März 1916"; Killinger, *Die Abenteuer des Ostseefliegers*, 18–31. Unless otherwise cited, the account of their treatment and movements in this chapter is taken from these two sources.
2. Brian K. Feltman, *The Stigma of Surrender: German Prisoners, British Captors, and Manhood in the Great War and Beyond* (Chapel Hill: University of North Carolina Press, 2015), 1, 13–36.
3. Ibid., 90–94.

Chapter 5. Prison

1. "Bericht des Leutnants zur See Killinger über seine Gefangennahme in Russland und Flucht aus Siberien, 11 März 1916"; Killinger, *Die Abenteuer des Ostseefliegers*, 31–46. All the material in this chapter is from these sources.

Chapter 6. Transported East

1. "Bericht des Leutnants zur See Killinger über seine Gefangennahme in Russland und Flucht aus Siberien, 11 März 1916"; Killinger, *Die Abenteuer des Ostseefliegers*, 46–58. Unless otherwise cited, the account of their treatment and movements in this chapter is from these two sources.
2. Berlin Command, Seventh Army, training syllabus, "Escape and Evasion," 22 typed pages, January 1959, and handwritten notes on lectures, films, and text taken by the author during training that included a practical field exercise.
3. Office of the Surgeon General, Col. Martha K. Lenhart, ed., *The Medical Aspects of Chemical Warfare* (Washington, D.C.: GPO, n.d.), 14; Marshall, *World War I*, 139–40, 156–57.
4. Georg Wurzer, "Die Kriegsgefangenen der Mittelmächte in Russland im Ersten Weltkrieg" (Ph.D. diss., University of Tübingen, 2000), 8. Wurzer notes that the use of passes to go out of the camp was fairly common in Siberian POW officers' camps early in the war, although the practice was limited to camps in remote locations.

Chapter 7. Escape

1. "Bericht des Leutnants zur See Killinger über seine Gefangennahme in Russland und Flucht aus Siberien, 11 März 1916"; Killinger, *Die Abenteuer des Ostseefliegers*, 58–71. Unless otherwise cited, the account of their movements and experiences in this chapter is from these two sources.
2. Sören Urbansky, *Kolonialer Wettstreit: Russland, China, Japan und die Ostchinesische Eisenbahn* (Frankfurt and New York: Campus Publishers, 2008), 98–127.
3. Some of the details and descriptions of the Trans-Siberian Railway from Omsk to Harbin are from Department of Railways, *Official Guide to Eastern Asia: Chosen, Manchuria, Siberia* (Tokyo, 1900), 27–23.
4. Kurt Cleinow, geb. 30 November 1894, "Flieger-Karteikarte," Bundesarchiv, Zentralnachweisstelle, Aachen, Germany; "Personalunterlagen für Kurt Cleinow," Deutsche Dienststelle für die Benachrichtigung der nächsten Angehörigen von Gefallenen der ehemaligen deutschen Wehrmacht, Berlin.

Chapter 8. Evasion

1. "Bericht des Leutnants zur See Killinger über seine Gefangennahme in Russland und Flucht aus Siberien, 11 März 1916"; "Erfahrungen des Leutnants zur See Killinger bei seiner Flucht aus Siberien, 13 März 1916," Records of the German Navy, 1850–1945, RG242, microfilm publication T1022, rolls 657 and 658, PG75191, National Archives II, College Park, Md. [hereafter "Erfahrungen des Leutnants zur See Killinger bei seiner Flucht aus Siberien, 13 März 1916"]; Killinger, *Die Abenteuer des Ostseefliegers*, 71–85. Unless otherwise noted, this account of their movements and experiences is taken from these sources.
2. Wurzer, "Die Kriegsgefangenen der Mittelmächte in Russland im Ersten Weltkrieg," 167.
3. A. R. Crawford, *Sketches of Missionary Life in Manchuria* (Belfast: R. Carswell & Son, 1899), 65; Yishi Liu and Xinying Wang, "A Pictorial History of Changchun, 1898–1962," *Cross-Currents: East Asian History and Culture Review*, no. 5 (December 2012): 190–96, http://cross-currents .berkeley.edu/sites/default/files/e-journal/photo-essays/liu_and_ wang_1.pdf. In both of his books Killinger calls this town "Mompanse."

Chapter 9. The Escape Pipeline

1. "Erfahrungen des Leutnants zur See Killinger bei seiner Flucht aus Siberien, 13 März 1916"; Killinger, *Die Abenteuer des Ostseefliegers*, 86–95. Unless otherwise cited, this account of their movements and experiences is taken from these two sources.
2. "Gesuch des Leutnants zur See Killinger um Rückerstattung der Kosten für seine Flucht aus Siberien, Berlin den 11 März 1916," microfilm publication T1022, rolls 657 and 658, PG75191, National Archives II, College Park, Md. [hereafter "Gesuch des Leutnants zur See Killinger," 11 März 1916].
3. Dwight R. Messimer, "German Gunboats on the Yangtse," *Naval History* 1, no. 1 (April 1987): 60; and Messimer, "Gunboats and Diplomats," *American Neptune* 40 (April 1980): 85–99.
4. "Gesuch des Leutnants zur See Killinger, 11 März 1916."
5. Gröner, *Die Deutschen Kriegsschiffe*, 31.
6. "Erfahrungen des Leutnants zur See Killinger bei seiner Flucht aus Siberien," 13 März 1916.
7. Franz Wlad, *Meine Flucht durchs mongolische Sandmeer* (Berlin: Ullstein Verlag, 1918), 187.
8. Ibid., 115–18.
9. Arno Spindler, *Der Handelskrieg mit U-Booten*, vol. 2 (Frankfurt a. M.: Verlag E. S. Mittler & Sohn, 1966): 38–40 and 247.
10. Karl E. Kassowitz, *Die Flucht um den Erdball: Erlebnisse eines österreichischen Militärarztes an der Front, in Sibirien, in Mandschukuo, und auf der Flucht um die Erde* (Leipzig Mährisch-Ostrau: Verlag Julius Kittls Nachfolger, 1936), 70, 144–45, 148, 154–55, 172–73.
11. Wlad, *Meine Flucht durchs mongolische Sandmeer*, 188, 199, 201, 206–7.
12. For a complete account of Etappendienst activity in San Francisco, see David H. Grover, *San Francisco Shipping Conspiracies of World War One* (Napa, Calif.: Western Maritime Press, 1995).

Chapter 10. Transpacific

1. Unless otherwise cited, this account is from "Bericht des Leutnants zur See Killinger über seine Erfahrungen in Japan und Amerika, 15 März 1916," Records of the German Navy, 1850–1945, RG242, microfilm publication T1022, rolls 657 and 658, PG75191, National Archives

II, College Park, Md. [hereafter "Bericht des Leutnants zur See Killinger über seine Erfahrungen in Japan und Amerika, 15 März 1916"]; and Killinger, *Die Abenteuer des Ostseefliegers*, 96–130.

2. "Gesuch des Leutnants zur See Killinger um Rückerstattung der Kosten für seine Flucht aus Siberien, 11 März 1916."
3. Grover, *San Francisco Shipping Conspiracies of World War One*, 96.

Chapter 11. Transcontinental USA

1. Killinger, *Die Abenteuer des Ostseefliegers*, 131–52; "Bericht des Leutnants zur See Killinger über seine Erfahrungen in Japan und Amerika, 15 März 1916." In his books Killinger provided an elaborate account of being physically assaulted by the press and having to flee the dock in a taxi. He made no mention of such a confrontation with the press in his official report.
2. Killinger, *Die Abenteuer des Ostseefliegers*, 131–32.
3. The story about Killinger appeared on the front page of a *San Francisco Call Bulletin* extra edition on 25 January. The *San Francisco Chronicle* ran a story on the front page of the 26 January edition about three French nationals from the *Shinyo Maru* whom the police arrested for smuggling diamonds. They might have been the alleged French opium smuggler and his female companions.
4. "Bericht des Leutnants zur See Killinger über seine Erfahrungen in Japan und Amerika, 15 März 1916"; "Gesuch des Leutnants zur See Killinger, 11 März 1916."
5. Melody C. Whitener Smith, "Harvey Girls Changed the West," El Paso, Texas, Community College Library, epcc.libguides.com/harveygirls.
6. Killinger, *Die Abenteuer des Ostseefliegers*, 140–41.
7. Ibid., 142–43.
8. "Bericht des Leutnants zur See Killinger über seine Erfahrungen in Japan und Amerika, 15 März 1916"; Killinger, *Die Abenteuer des Ostseefliegers*, 141–67. Unless otherwise noted, this typewritten report and his 1934 book are the sources for the account and quotes that follow.
9. "Bericht des Leutnants zur See Killinger über seine Erfahrungen in Japan und Amerika, 15 März 1916"; "Gesuch des Leutnants zur See Killinger, um Rückerstattung der Kosten für seine Flucht aus Siberien, 11 März 1916."
10. Killinger, *Die Abenteuer des Ostseefliegers*, 151–52.

Chapter 12. Transatlantic

1. "Bericht des Leutnants zur See Killinger über seine Erfahrungen in Japan und Amerika, 15 März 1916"; Killinger, *Die Abenteuer des Ostseefliegers*, 153–76. All the material in this chapter is from these sources.

Chapter 13. Germany

1. Fernando Esposito, ed., *Mythische Moderne: Aviatik, Faschismus und die Sehnsucht nach Ordnung in Deutschland und Italien* (Oldenburg: Oldenburg Verlag, 2011), 174–75, 181.
2. "Admiralstab to Kiel, 19 August 1916, and Kommando Marinestation Nordsee an Admiralstab, 28 März 1918," Records of the German Navy, 1850–1945, RG242, microfilm publication T1022, roll 658, PG75191, National Archives II, College Park, Md.
3. Johan Ryheul, *Marinekorps Flandern, 1914–1918* (Hamburg, Berlin, Bonn: E. S. Mittler & Sohn, GmbH, 1997), 112.
4. Alfred F. B. Carpenter, "The Zeebrugge Affair," in *Canadian Club Yearbook, 1918–1919* (Ottawa: Dadson-Merrill Press, 1919), 85.
5. Ryheul, *Marinekorps Flandern*, 124; Alfred F. B. Carpenter, *The Blocking of Zeebrugge* (London: Herbert Jenkins, 1925), 30.
6. Neal W. O'Connor, *Aviation Awards of Imperial Germany in World War I and the Men Who Earned Them* (Princeton: Flying Machine Press, 1999), no page, provided by Rick Lundstrom, Oxford, Miss.
7. Bodo Herzog, *Deutsche U-Boote, 1906–1966* (Koblenz: Pawlak, 1990), 136–42.
8. Sir Roger Keyes, *The Naval Memoirs of Admiral of the Fleet Sir Rodger Keyes*, 2 vols. (New York: E. P. Dutton, 1934–1935), 2:257–92.
9. Ibid., 295.
10. Henry Newbolt, *Naval Operations*, 5 vols. (London, New York, Toronto: Longmans, Green, 1920–31), 5:265.
11. Ibid., 364.
12. Ryheul, *Marinekorps Flandern*, 239–41.
13. Newbolt, *Naval Operations*, 5:369–70; Spindler, *Der Handelskrieg mit U-Booten*, 5:5, 338.
14. Spindler, *Der Handelskrieg mit U-Booten*, 5:338, 340.

15. Stefan Geck, *Dulag Luft, Auswertestelle West: Vernehmungslager der Luftwaffe für westalliierte Kriegsgefangene in Zweiten Weltkrieg* (Frankfurt: Peter Lang GmbH, 2008), 84–85.

16. Ibid.

Chapter 14. War Criminal

1. Tim Carroll, *The Great Escape from Stalag Luft III* (New York, London, Toronto, Sydney: Pocket Books, 2004), 55.

2. Norman L. R. Franks, Frank W. Bailey, and Russell Guest, *Above the Lines* (London: Grub Street, 1993), 36–40, 94.

3. Carroll, *The Great Escape*, 54–55.

4. Eric Cuddon, ed., *The Dulag Luft Trial* (London: William Hodge, 1952), 143. Unless otherwise noted, the material in this chapter is from this source.

5. Stefan Geck, *Dulag Luft, Auswertestelle West: Vernehmungslager der Luftwaffe für westalliierte Kriegsgefangene in zweiten Weltkrieg* (Frankfurt: Peter Lang GmbH, 2008), 89.

6. Todesanzeige, Erich Killinger, *Marineforum* (August 1977), provided by Holger Hoffmann, *Marineforum*, Organ der Marine-Offizier-Vereinigung, Bonn.

Bibliography

Published Works

Air Ministry, Great Britain. *Handbook of German Military and Naval Aviation (War)*. London: HMSO, October 1918.

"Aircraft and the War." *Flight*, 5 February 1915.

Carpenter, Alfred F. B. *The Blocking of Zeebrugge*. New York and London: Herbert Jenkins, 1925.

———. "The Zeebrugge Affair." In *Canadian Club Yearbook, 1918–1919*. Ottawa: Dadson-Merrill Press, 1919, 83–101.

Carroll, Tim. *The Great Escape from Stalag Luft III*. New York, London, Toronto, and Sydney: Pocket Books, 2004.

Crawford, A. R. *Sketches of Missionary Life in Manchuria; Being Extracts from Letters Home of Rev. A. R. Crawford, Missionary of the Irish Presbyterian Church*. Belfast: A. R. Crawford & Son, 1899.

Cuddon, Eric, ed. *The Dulag Luft Trial*. London: William Hodge, 1952.

Department of Modern Languages, U.S. Naval Academy. *Spanish Nautical Phrase Book and Reader*. "Table of Comparative Ranks in Different Navies." Annapolis: U.S. Naval Institute, 1914.

Department of Railways. *Official Guide to Eastern Asia: Chosen, Manchuria, Siberia*. Tokyo, 1900.

Eberhardt, Walter von, ed. *Unsere Luftstreitkräfte, 1914–1918*. 2 vols. Berlin: Vaterlandischer Verlag C. A. Weller, 1930.

Esposito, Fernando, ed. *Mythische Moderne: Aviatik, Faschismus und die Sehnsucht nach Ordnung in Deutschland und Italien*. Oldenburg: Oldenburg Verlag, 2011.

Feltman, Brian K. *The Stigma of Surrender: German Prisoners, British Captors, and Manhood in the Great War and Beyond*. Chapel Hill: University of North Carolina Press, 2015.

Firle, Rudolph. *Der Krieg in der Ostsee*. 3 vols. In *Der Krieg zur See 1914–1918*, gen. ed. Eberhard von Mantey. Berlin: Verlag E. S. Mittler & Sohn, 1922.

Franks, Norman L. R., Frank W. Bailey, and Rick Duiven. *The Jasta Pilots*. London: Grub Street, 1996.

Franks, Norman L. R., Frank W. Bailey, and Russell Guest. *Above the Lines.* London: Grub Street, 1993.

Geck, Stefan. *Dulag Luft, Auswertestelle West: Vernehmungslager der Luftwaffe für westalliierte Kriegsgefangene in Zweiten Weltkrieg.* Frankfurt: Peter Lang GmbH, 2008.

Gröner, Erich. *Die Deutschen Kriegsschiffe, 1815–1945.* 2 vols. Munich: J. F. Lehmanns Verlag, 1966.

Groos, Otto. *Der Krieg in der Nordsee.* 7 vols. In *Der Krieg zur See 1914–1918,* gen. ed. Eberhard von Mantey. Berlin: Verlag E. S. Mittler & Sohn, 1922.

Grover, David H. *San Francisco Shipping Conspiracies of World War One.* Napa, Calif.: Western Maritime Press, 1995.

Gunston, Bill. *World Encyclopedia of Aircraft Manufacturers.* Annapolis: Naval Institute Press, 1993.

Halpern, Paul G. *A Naval History of World War I.* Annapolis: Naval Institute Press, 1994.

Herzog, Bodo. *Deutsche U-Boote, 1906–1966.* Koblenz: Pawlak, 1990.

Jung, Dieter, Martin Maas, and Berndt Wenzel. *Tanker und Versorger der deutschen Flotte, 1900–1980.* Stuttgart: Motorbuch Verlag, 1981.

Jung, Dieter, Berndt Wenzel, and Arno Abendroth. *Die Schiffe und Boote der deutschen Seeflieger, 1912–1976.* Stuttgart: Motorbuch Verlag, 1977.

Kassowitz, Karl E. *Die Flucht um den Erdball: Erlebnisse eines österreichischen Militärarztes an der Front, in Sibirien, in Mandschukuo, und auf der Flucht um die Erde.* Leipzig, Mährisch, and Ostrau: Verlag Julius Kittls Nachfolger, 1936.

Keyes, Sir Roger. *The Naval Memoirs of Admiral of the Fleet Sir Rodger Keyes.* 2 vols. New York: E. P. Dutton, 1934–35.

Killinger, Erich. *Die Abenteuer des Ostfliegers.* Berlin: Ullstein, 1917.

———. *Flucht um die Erde: Die Abenteuer des Ostfliegers.* Berlin: Im Deutschen Verlag, 1934.

Knox, Major General Sir Alfred. *With the Russian Army, 1914–1917: Being Chiefly Extracts from the Diary of a Military Attaché.* London: Hutchenson, 1921.

Liu, Yishi, and Xinying Wang. "A Pictorial History of Changchun, 1898–1962." *Cross-Currents: East Asian History and Culture Review* (University of California, Berkeley), no. 5 (December 2012): 190–217. http://cross-currents.berkeley.edu/sites/default/files/e-journal/photo-essays/liu_and_wang_1.pdf.

Marshall, S. L. A. *World War I*. New York: American Heritage Press, 1971.

Messimer, Dwight R. *Escape*. Annapolis: Naval Institute Press, 1994.

———. *Escape from Villingen, 1918*. College Station: Texas A&M University Press, 2000.

———. "German Gunboats on the Yangtse." *Naval History* 1, no. 1. (1987): 57–63.

———. "Gunboats and Diplomats." *American Neptune* 40, no. 2 (1980): 85–99.

Morrow, John Howard Jr. *Building German Airpower, 1909–1914*. Knoxville: University of Tennessee Press, 1976.

Newbolt, Henry. *Naval Operations*. 5 vols. London, New York, and Toronto: Longmans, Green, 1920–31.

O'Connor, Neal W. *Aviation Awards of Imperial Germany in World War I and the Men Who Earned Them*. Princeton, N.J.: Flying Machine Press, 1999. Provided by Richard Lundstrom, Oxford, Miss.

Office of the Surgeon General. *The Medical Aspects of Chemical Warfare*, ed. Col. Martha K. Lenhart. Washington, D.C.: GPO, no date. http://www.cs.amedd.army.mil/borden/Portlet.aspx?id=d3d11f5a-f2ef-4b4e-b75b-6ba4b64e4fb2.

Rollmann, Heinrich. *Der Krieg in der Ostsee*. 3 vols. In *Der Krieg zur See 1914–1918*, gen. ed. Eberhard von Mantey. Berlin: Verlag E. S. Mittler & Sohn, 1929.

Rumpler Werke. *Rumpler Zehn Jahre Deutsche Flugtechnik*. Berlin: Echsteins Biographischer Verlag, 1921.

Ryheul, Johan. *Marinekorps Flandern, 1914–1918*. Hamburg, Berlin, and Bonn: E. S. Mittler & Sohn, GmbH, 1997.

Spindler, Arno. *Der Handelskrieg mit U-Booten*. 5 vols. In *Der Krieg zur See 1914–1918*, gen. ed. Eberhard von Mantey. Frankfurt a. M.: Verlag E. S. Mittler & Sohn, 1966.

Toliver, Raymond F. *The Interrogator*. Atglen, Pa.: Schiffer, 1997.

Urbansky, Sören. *Kolonialer Wettstreit: Russland, China, Japan und die Ostchinesische Eisenbahn*. Frankfurt and New York: Campus Publishers, 2008.

Wlad, Franz. *Meine Flucht durchs mongolische Sandmeer*. Berlin: Ullstein, 1918.

German Archival Documents

Cleinow, Kurt. Geb. 30 October 1894. "Flieger-Karteikarte." Bundesarchiv, Zentralnachweisstelle, Aachen, Germany.

Ehrenrangliste der Kaiserlichen-Marine, 1914–1918. Bibliothek für Zeitgeschichte, Stuttgart.

Gorrissen, Karl von. Geb. 4 October 1888. "Flieger-Karteikarte." Bundesarchiv, Zentralnachweisstelle, Aachen, Germany.

Killinger, Erich. Geb. 21 März 1893. "Flieger-Karteikarte." Bundesarchiv, Zentralnachweisstelle, Aachen, Germany.

"Personalunterlagen für Clifford von Tempsky." Deutsche Dienststelle für die Benachrichtigung der nächsten Angehörigen von Gefallenen der ehemaligen deutschen Wehrmacht, Berlin.

"Personalunterlagen für Erich Killinger." Deutsche Dienststelle für die Benachrichtigung der nächsten Angehörigen von Gefallenen der ehemaligen deutschen Wehrmacht, Berlin.

"Personalunterlagen für Karl von Gorrissen." Deutsche Dienststelle für die Benachrichtigung der nächsten Angehörigen von Gefallenen der ehemaligen deutschen Wehrmacht, Berlin.

"Personalunterlagen für Kurt Cleinow." Deutsche Dienststelle für die Benachrichtigung der nächsten Angehörigen von Gefallenen der ehemaligen deutschen Wehrmacht, Berlin.

Tempsky, Clifford von. Geb. 1 März 1891. "Flieger-Karteikarte." Bundesarchiv, Zentralnachweisstelle, Aachen, Germany.

U.S. Archival Documents

"Admiralstab to Kiel, 19 August 1916." Records of the German Navy, RG242, microfilm publication T1022, PG67344. National Archives II, College Park, Md.

"Bericht des Leutnants zur See Killinger über seine Erfahrungen in Japan und Amerika, 15 März 1916." Records of the German Navy, 1850–1945, RG242, microfilm publication T1022, rolls 657 and 658, PG75191. National Archives II, College Park, Md.

"Bericht des Leutnants zur See Killinger über seine Gefangennahme in Russland und Flucht aus Siberien, 11 März 1916." Records of the German Navy, 1850–1945, RG242, microfilm publication T1022, rolls 657 and 658, PG75191. National Archives II, College Park, Md.

"Erfahrungen des Leutnants zur See Killinger bei seiner Flucht aus Siberien, 13 März 1916." Records of the German Navy, 1850–1945, RG242, microfilm publication T1022, rolls 657 and 658, PG75191. National Archives II, College Park, Md.

"Gesuch des Leutnants zur See Killinger um Rückerstattung der Kosten für seine Flucht aus Siberien, 11 März 1916." Records of the German

Navy, 1850–1945, RG242, microfilm publication T1022, rolls 657 and 658, PG75191. National Archives II, College Park, Md.

"Kommando Marinestation Nordsee an Admiralstab, 28 March 1918." RG242, Records of the German Navy, 1850–1945, microfilm publication T1022, rolls 657 and 658, PG75191. National Archives II, College Park, Md.

Military Intelligence Service. "Dulag Luft," 15 July 1944 and 1 November 1945. RG338, Records of U.S. Army Operational, Tactical, and Support Organizations (World War II and thereafter).

———. "Transit Camp, Section of Dulag Luft," 1 November 1945. RG338, Records of U.S. Army Operational, Tactical, and Support Organizations (World War II and thereafter).

Unpublished Works

Wurzer, Georg. "Die Kriegsgefangenen der Mittelmächte in Russland im Ersten Weltkrieg." Ph.D. dissertation, University of Tübingen, 2000.

Correspondence

"Crew IV/1913" a class roster with school ship assignments; and "Eintrag, Erich Killinger" a service record, 1913–1945. Provided by Joachim Scherneck-Czech, Archivassistent im Wehrgeschichtlichen Ausbildungszentrum der Marineschule Mürwik, Kelmstrasse 14 D-24944 Flensburg.

"Erich Walter Emil Killinger Biografie." Provided by Klaus Liedtke. Bibliothek-Archiv, Marine-Offizier-Vereinigung, Ulrich-von-Hassell-Str. 2, D-53123 Bonn, Germany.

Todesanzeige, Clifford von Tempsky. *Marineforum* (February 1961). Provided by Holger Hoffmann, *Marineforum*, Organ der Marine-Offizier-Vereinigung, Bonn.

Todesanzeige, Erich Killinger. *Marineforum* (August 1977). Provided by Holger Hoffmann, *Marineforum* Organ der Marine-Offizier-Vereinigung, Bonn.

Todesanzeige, Karl von Gorrissen. *Marineforum* (February 1919). Provided by Holger Hoffmann, *Marineforum* Organ der Marine-Offizier-Vereinigung, Bonn.

Index

Die Abenteuer des Ostseefliegers (Killinger), 47, 138, 169
Ackermann, Jacob, 162
Adelung, Wilhelm, 2–3
airships, 8, 18. *See also* Parseval PL-19 airship
Albatros W.4 fighters, 141
Alisov, Mikhail, 61
Appam (Great Britain), 124
Ascot (Great Britain), 146
Asian-European land route to Germany, 93–94
Augsburg (Germany), 13, 36
Austria: Austria-Hungary, declaration of war against Serbia, 3; escaped POWs in Kirin, arrest and internment of, 83; Franz Ferdinand murder and start of World War I, 3; German army units sent to support, 54–55; Killinger hiking trip to against commandant's orders, 3–4; mobilization orders for reservists in, 4; POWs at Omsk camp, 54, 56; POWs at Udinsk camp, 58–60; sea route of POWs back to, 95–96; Seven Weeks War, 7; telegram ordering Killinger return to school, 3–4; train back to Germany from, 4–5
Auswertestelle West. *See* Dulag Luft camp
aviation industry: aircraft contracts, aviation industry preference for army, 8; Johannisthal location for design and manufacturing companies, 9; Killinger employment in during interwar period, 146–47; naval aircraft designs, difficulty and expense of building, 8

Bachmann, Rolf, 10, 20
Bain, Victor Albert, 159–60
Baltic Coastal Defense Division, 5
Baltic naval force (Germany): aircraft assigned to, number and status of, 10; disruption of Russian retreat, orders for, 12; Heinrich command of, 10; Killinger assignment to, 10; Libau blockage and shelling, orders for, 15; Memel occupation by Russian, response to probable, 15; patrol operations in Baltic Sea, 13–16; patrol operations to learn movements of Russian fleet, 14–15; pilots in, training and experience of, 10; reservists assignments to, 10; ships and units assigned to, 10, 12; transfer from, Killinger requests for, 12–13
Baltic Sea and region: British submarines in, 14, 15; fighter opposition in, lack of, 10; German operations to open for trade, 12; German patrol operations in, 13–16; map of, 11; minelaying and minesweeping operations in, 10; Pillau base on and World War II assignment, 147–48; reconnaissance patrols from *Glyndwr*, 17, 18–23, 24–25; Russian operations in, 13–16; sea war in, 12; secondary theater of operations status of, 10, 12; shore bombardment operations in, 10; special operations to draw Russia into skirmishes in, 13; training missions over, 11
Baltimore: address for getting counterfeit passport in, 119–20, 124; *Storfield* passage to Norway from, 125–34; train to and accommodations in, 124–25
Barnes, Albert Tom, 164–65
Bartolome, Walter, 3–4
Bauer-Schlichtegroll, Gustav, 152–53, 155–56, 162, 163, 166
Baumgartner, Heinrich, 93, 97, 98, 99–100, 105, 106, 109
Behring, Ehler: chief of special operations assignment, 13; detached admiral title of, 13; experience and skills of, 13; *Glyndwr* conversion to tender and barracks ship, 16; Libau blockage

Chinese soldier, 81–82; discussions with interpreter about Chinese soldier and Europeans in, 82–83; escaped POWs in, arrest and internment of, 83; interpreter as known informer, 83; raids and search by Chinese officials in, 83–84; trip to, 78–82
Knight's Cross of the Military Karl Friedrich Merit-Order, 142
Königsberg, 11, 17, 19, 51
Kronprinz Wilhelm (Germany), 130–31
Kuriches Haff, 18–23

Lang, Robert T., 156–57
Laurence, Noel F., 14
Lehmann, Ernst: age and physical condition of, 70; clothing, money, and identity papers for, 86, 87–88; ferryman, paying of by, 80–81; jump from train, 73; order for jumping from train, 72; pairing with Brunn and departure for Tientsin, 88; POW at hotel/camp, 47; railcar transport to Siberia, 51; return to Germany by land route, 94; role in escape group from train, 69; shooting down of, 47, 69
Libau: air raids on and shelling of, 17–18, 31, 36; antiaircraft defenses at, 25, 171n4; block ships to close harbor at, 13, 16, 24; British submarines based in, false report on, 14, 15; British submarines orders to for refueling, 14; *Friedrich Carl*, seaplanes, and crews for raid on, 16; German attack on, preparations for, 14; German blockage and shelling of, orders for, 15; map of, 11; PL-19 air raid on, 17–18, 31, 51; POWs arrival in and placement in railcar, 34; reconnaissance patrols of Killinger and von Gorrisen to, 16, 17, 18–23, 24–25; Russian evacuation from, 13–14; Russian naval base at, speculation about, 13; Russian retreat from Memel toward, 18; train station bombing, questioning about, 30–31, 35, 36, 40, 45–46
library book communication system, 43–44
Lübeck (Germany), 21, 24, 27, 36
Lübeck Hanseatic Cross, 140

Luftwaffe: Coastal Aviation Group 506 assignment, 147–48; commissioning in Luftwaffe Reserve, 147; court-martial of Killinger, 152; headquarters staff assignment, 148; Polish campaign, 148. *See also* Dulag Luft camp

Magdeburg (Germany), 24, 36
Manchuria, 65–67, 72, 77, 83. *See also* Changchun; Kirin
Marinekorps: British raids on U-boat bases, 142–45; evacuation of Flanders by, 145–46; missions of, 142; protection of U-boats of, 142–43
Masurian Lakes, First Battle of the, 11–12, 54
Masurian Lakes, Second Battle of the, 55
medical treatment: demand for, 44–45; withholding of, 49–50; withholding of and war crimes charges, 153, 162–65
Meier, Ernst, 17, 18, 48, 51, 53
Memel: block ships to close harbor at, 15; *Glyndwr* as coaling station in, 16; map of, 11; naval infantryman taking prisoner in, 49; pontoon bridges between Tilsit and, 12; reconnaissance patrols to Libau from, 16, 18–23, 24–25; Russian attack on, 18; Russian occupation of, German response to probable, 15; Russian retreat from, 18; sinking of *Friedrich Carl* off coast of, 36, 45; spy captured near, 18
Memel River pontoon bridges, 12
Menche, Heinz, 21
Mexican silver coins, 88, 92, 101
minefields, minelaying, and minesweeping operations, 10, 11, 14
Mongolia, 70–72
Möwe (Germany), 124
Mukden: American consulate in, directions to, 83, 87; bandits between Changchun and, 78; branches of railways to, 78–80, 84–85; departure from after reports in newspaper about escapees, 88; escape at Harbin and plans to catch southbound train to, 67; escape before Harbin and walk south to, 68; freight wagon trip to, 84–85; German consulate in, access to by escapees because of location, 87;

About the Author

Dwight R. Messimer was raised in California. As a soldier, he was stationed in Berlin where he married his wife, Renate, in 1959. Following his discharge in 1962 he traveled frequently to Germany for historical research, obtained his Master's degree in history, and was a sergeant in the San Jose Police Department and history professor at San Jose State University. Messimer has been writing for publication since 1979. He has been an invited speaker at the Great War Society, Johns Hopkins University Applied Physics Lab, Military Operations Research Society, National Archives, Naval Postgraduate School, Naval War College, and the Submarine Forces School. He lives with his wife in northern California.